This book will lead and guide you on the path of life's success and salvation. Get ready for a complete turn-around for the best in the journey of your life.

—REVEREND DR. JAMES G. SALAKO
PASTOR / GENERAL OVERSEER
CHRIST BIBLE CHURCH
COLUMBUS, OHIO

From the very day a child is born, to the day he goes to meet his Maker, his life's journey is established. No one came to this world by chance. Everyone is created by God for a definite purpose. However, how we comport or conduct ourselves will determine whether we will live to fully experience all that God has destined or fall short of His plans. With a sharp sense of clarity, Yomi enunciates the avoidable pitfalls that could easily cut short the perfect plan of God. He shares his view from a perspective which men rarely see in this lifetime. Take time to meditate on the salient truths as you read, and you will be greatly blessed.

—PASTOR SAM ADEYEMI
SENIOR PASTOR
OVERCOMERS' CHRISTIAN CENTER
COLUMBUS, OHIO

Read this book and learn how to avoid the path to Pisgah. You can choose God's incredible destiny for your life. Find out how God's grace is sufficient for your life and how He will empower you to do great things for Him. Make no excuses. Meet the Almighty on the pages of *Avoid the Path to Pisgah* and find your greatest dreams realized for your life.

—JANET HOLM MCHENRY
SPEAKER AND AUTHOR OF TWENTY BOOKS,
INCLUDING *PRAYERWALK* AND *PRAYERSTREAMING*

AVOID
the PATH

to
Pisgah

Zaeh & Juliet,
May this be a blessing to you,
Yomi Akinyemi

ABAYOMI
AKINYEMI

CREATION HOUSE
A STRANG COMPANY

Avoid the Path to Pisgah by Abayomi Akinyemi
Published by Creation House
A Strang Company
600 Rinehart Road
Lake Mary, Florida 32746
www.creationhouse.com

Unless otherwise noted, all Scripture quotations are from the New American Standard Bible. Copyright © 1960, 1962, 1963, 1968, 1971, 1972, 1973, 1975, 1977 by the Lockman Foundation. Used by permission. (www.Lockman.org)

Scripture quotations marked NIV are from the Holy Bible, New International Version of the Bible. Copyright © 1973, 1978, 1984, International Bible Society. Used by permission.

Scripture quotations marked KJV are from the King James Version of the Bible.

English definitions are from www.dictionary.com.

Design Director: Bill Johnson
Cover design by Amanda Potter

Library of Congress Control Number: 2008923860
International Standard Book Number: 978-1-59979-354-2

First Edition

08 09 10 11 12 — 9 8 7 6 5 4 3 2 1
Printed in the United States of America

This book is dedicated to the Lord almighty—the One who is faithful to His words and is in charge of the affairs of men. May His name be glorified forever.

CONTENTS

ACKNOWLEDGMENTS

I THANK THE LORD who inspired me to write this book. He has proved once again that He can use anyone. I am indeed humbled and privileged to be used of Him.

I thank my wife, Toyin for her love, understanding, suggestions, and contributions to this book. My love, I am so thankful to God for blessing me with you. I also thank my kids for their understanding when Daddy was not there to spend as much time as I ordinarily would love to during the course of writing this book.

I thank my parents Deacon S. Olayiwola and Deaconess Olufunke A. Akinyemi for all the spiritual values imparted to me, and my parents-in-law, Mr. Godwin O. and Mrs. Comfort Adenike Oyekunle (of blessed memory) who also took me as their own child, supported, and believed in me from the very beginning.

I thank Janet Holm McHenry for being such an inspiration to me. Your suggestions and personal contribution to this book cannot be overemphasized. You are indeed God-sent, and I cannot thank you enough. May the Lord reward you a million-fold.

I thank Pastor Sam Adeyemi, Pastor Femi Oyewusi, James and Beatrice Ogundimu, Dr. Felix and Feyi Tolani, Reverend Ray and Joy Murray, William and Ingrid Shepherd, Reverend Dr. James Salako, Dona Eveatt, and Pastor Femi and Folake Gbenjo for their support and encouragement when they were needed most. May the Lord continue to make you a blessing.

Finally, I thank the staff at Strang Communications for their help and cooperation at making sure that this book is published. May the Lord continue to enlarge your territory.

FOREWORD

WHEN I WAS a senior in college, I knew that God had called me to work for the publishing arm of a national ministry that worked with college students. I had my application approved and ready to mail just before Christmas break when fear overcame me. I wondered to myself, "How would I raise support? Wasn't asking for money like begging? What would others think of me if I asked them to fund my job? Would I end up on a deserted island instead of the publishing office?" With those doubts I left my application in my dorm room and headed home for the holidays. Just a few days later my boyfriend asked me to marry him. Since I figured he would be a rich lawyer someday, I decided my future was safer in his hands than in God's.

Thirteen years and three babies later, I found myself discontent. I had a husband who loved me, a beautiful home, and three great kids, but my life seemed purposeless. One day I told God that I was giving him everything—my family, my husband, myself, all that I had—and would follow His lordship and destiny for my life. I remember praying: "Even if that means going to a deserted island without a single thing!" I was ready to do His will in my life. A short time later I sensed His call to me again: *I want you to write for me.* I had no idea what that meant, but I stepped out in faith and began trusting Him to use me. That was twenty years ago, and now I have written twenty books.

Abayomi Akinyemi writes about how we can avoid missing God's perfect destiny for our lives, framed around Moses' choice to climb Mount Pisgah to view the Promised Land instead of following God's leading. As a result, Moses missed seeing the fruition of his forty years of leading the Israelites through the desert. His destiny blows away like the sand in the wind, simply because he thought he knew better than God did.

At a writer's conference many years after God's graceful second call to me, I got a glimpse of what I had missed those intermittent thirteen years when I met the man who would have been my boss at the publishing arm of the campus ministry. As he explained to our class about how he moved into writing books, I knew deeply in my heart that I could have been doing the same many years earlier—and felt the peace of knowing I was living in God's will all those intervening years. Were my marriage and children in God's perfect will? Yes, God did give me peace about that—but I had pushed God's schedule for my life out of whack. And just for the record, my husband Craig is now a poor farmer instead of a rich attorney! But we are both happier because we're both doing what God has called us to.

You are at a crossroads in your life. You can choose God's incredible destiny for your life—or you can follow your own leanings. It won't be easy. God may want to move you out of your comfort zone. And you may feel like hiding from Him. The enemy will have an endless stream of distractions—wonderful Pisgah lookouts that seem so appealing and so right. But you can't outrun God. He has pursued you for generations and His way is best.

Read this book and learn how to avoid the road to Pisgah. Find out how God's grace is sufficient for your life and how He will empower you to do great things for Him. Make no excuses.

Meet the Almighty on the pages of *Avoid the Path to Pisgah* and find your greatest dreams realized for your life.

—JANET HOLM MCHENRY
SPEAKER AND AUTHOR OF TWENTY BOOKS,
INCLUDING *PRAYERWALK* AND *PRAYERSTREAMING*

INTRODUCTION

I T WAS VERY hot and humid on this particular day in the month of April of 1999 in Lagos, Nigeria, West Africa. April is about the last month of the dry season and usually a very hot month in southwestern Nigeria, with temperatures ranging from 91 to 101 degrees. Surrounded by the Atlantic Ocean, Victoria Island, Lagos—where my office is located—is mostly a residential area with several palatial mansions. Traffic conditions on the streets that day were as chaotic as ever. Lagos is notorious for its traffic problems. Sometimes it takes more than two hours to commute a thirty-mile distance. If you happen to be out on a really bad day, it could take much longer. However, the conditions in the office this particular day were contrary to what was going on in the streets—the air conditioner was on as usual, operating probably at maximum capacity. It was calm and quiet, and to me it was just another day, but that would soon change. All of a sudden I heard one of my colleagues call my name. "Yomi, you have a phone call!"

"Who is it?" I asked.

"Your brother from America," he answered.

I dashed across the office to where the telephone was and grabbed it. "Hello, hello," I said, panting like a deer. It was my second cousin who lives in the US.

I greeted in Yoruba, my language, "*E kaa san,*" which means good afternoon.

"Congratulations," he said. "You have won the green card lottery." The green card lottery is organized every year by the

US State Department for several countries throughout the world. Millions apply worldwide from their countries of residence and only fifty-five thousand visas are made available. The selection is random according to the registration information, but once you are selected and complete the interview process at the US embassy in your resident country, you become an automatic permanent resident upon arrival in the US.

"Are you serious?" I asked.

"I have your winning notification with me," he said.

"Hallelujah!" I was overwhelmed with joy and disbelief at the same time, even shivering at that point. The joy that I felt that day was indescribable. The news came at a time in my life when the future seemed uncertain. At twenty-nine with a bachelor's degree and a post-graduate diploma, I only had a temporary job. While I was engaged to a beautiful twenty-six-year-old Christian lady, we lacked the resources to marry. Waiting was heartbreaking, but we continued trusting the Lord for a miracle. Then, from nowhere, it came—the assurance of living in the wealthiest nation in the universe without struggling to obtain a visa.

Many people had spent their life savings just to obtain an American visa in Nigeria without success. Many Nigerians had spent the night in front of the American embassy just to be able to get in line on time when the embassy opened the next morning. The majority had gone home disappointed as visa requests were denied. Corruption had eaten deep into the fabric of the Nigerian society and, while the country flowed with "milk and honey" as one of the largest producers of crude oil in the world, it was unable to cater to the needs of its citizenry. As a result, crime was rampant and many people, including the rich, lived in fear because of the security situation at the time.

Life can be very scary when one has no hope of a better future. I have been there.

There is nothing more frightening to me than a feeling of absolute helplessness. It gets even scarier when I have an urgent need and do not have any idea as to how the need will be met, or when I have a problem and have no hint as to how it will be solved. I hate to see problems come my way; I like everything to be perfect even though I live in this imperfect world. But the truth is that God has not promised His children a problem-free life. Instead, He said in James 1:2–4, "Consider it all joy, my brethren, when you encounter various trials, knowing that the testing of your faith produces endurance. And let endurance have its perfect result, so that you may be perfect and complete, lacking in nothing." Those challenging places are exactly where I find there is no other choice but to place my situation totally in God's hands.

Challenges that come our way as believers are designed to make us grow and propel us to greater heights in our relationship with Christ. Such challenges also are designed as steppingstones to God's divine blessings and provisions, and therefore are meant to be overcome. That is why the Bible also says in James 1:12, "Blessed is the man who perseveres under trial, because when he has stood the test, he will receive the crown of life that God has promised to those who love him" (NIV). On the contrary, we often become victims of our circumstances. We focus our attention on our situation rather than on Christ. We yield control to such situations and give up too soon, and the result of that is usually a destiny diverted or missed totally.

A road is often described as a course or path. The choice of road is so very important, because it determines whether or not we will get to our destination. We will see in this book how Moses chose the path to Pisgah—the viewing point on a plateau overlooking the Promised Land—and never arrived at his destination. Moses' dream of leading the Israelites to the Promised Land was unrealized—he was only able to view the land from the top of Pisgah. The reality today is that just like Moses, many Christians have their divine destiny frustrated, cut short, or totally destroyed as a result of their ignorance of the devil's schemes.

Avoid the Path to Pisgah is an eye opener as to how the devil seeks to cut short or destroy the destiny of every believer. He does this by using seemingly minor distractions, weaknesses, and temptations (described in the book as, "pathways to Pisgah"), as seen in the life of Moses. The significance of the metaphor of Pisgah as it applies to the life of a believer actually represents the following:

- A place where destiny is cut short or destroyed

- A place of unrealized dreams

- A place where passionate plea is no longer appreciated

- A place of failure at the edge of breakthrough

- A place of losing the fruits of one's labor

- A place of substitution or replacement

While it is possible that the spirit of Pisgah can crawl into your life as a believer, it is my intent through this book to show how you can defeat it, live victoriously, and pursue God's exciting plans for your life. This book also provides a special prayer for you to pray at the end of each chapter, based on the

Word of God—one that will guide you to freedom from past and potential mistakes.

The Word of the Lord says, "My people are destroyed for lack of knowledge" (Hosea 4:6). It is my prayer that you will gain knowledge that will help you on your spiritual journey. I pray this book will bless your life as you read it prayerfully. I believe your eyes will be opened and you will never be the same—in Jesus' name.

one

THE BIRTH OF A DESTINY

I N THE HEART of man is a void to be filled. There is a hunger from which man seeks a connection with a higher power. From Africa to Europe, the Americas to New Zealand, and from Asia to the Middle East there is a constant desire to know God. The situation in our world today could be likened to what the apostle Paul saw in Athens. The Bible says:

> So Paul stood in the midst of the Areopagus and said, "Men of Athens, I observe that you are very religious in all respects. For while I was passing through and examining the objects of your worship, I also found an altar with this inscription, 'TO AN UNKNOWN GOD.' Therefore what you worship in ignorance, this I proclaim to you."
>
> —ACTS 17:22–23

The people of Athens were very religious; they worshiped anything, even to the extent of dedicating an entire altar to an unknown god. The situation is the same in our current world. We worship all kinds of gods, but the truth of the matter is that there is only one God—the living God.

It is so easy for people in the church to blame others who worship idols, but being religious is not a substitute for being on the side of the living God. There are many in the church who may be serving an unknown god. I have always believed in the living God. At least, I thought I did. I went to church every Sunday and behaved in a manner that was consistent with the norms of the society where I lived, yet I did not truly know God. I saw God as a merciful and loving God who had no desire to punish anyone, no matter what. I often asked the question, "Of what profit would it be to God if He cast all the people who did not know Him into hellfire?" I used to think it would be a loss to God if He did that.

I thought I knew Him well enough, but it turned out I did not. Even though God is merciful and loving, what I did not know was that the same God that I thought I knew is also a just and holy God. I knew His Word that says His mercy endures forever, but ignored His Word that says, "Follow peace with all men, and holiness, without which no man shall see the Lord" (Heb. 12:14, KJV). Holiness is one of the attributes of the God that I claimed to serve, yet my life was nowhere close to being holy. I wanted to serve God and at the same time live my life the way it pleased me. The reality is that no unclean thing can come near God and it is only by the blood of Jesus that we can be saved.

How many people claim that they know God—just like I did—even in the church, yet have not had an encounter with Him? We hold malice against other people, yet claim to serve the God who despises malice. We live a double life, yet claim to serve the God who hates hypocrisy. (See Matthew 23:27–28.) Many more engage in acts of a sinful nature, yet claim to serve a God who says those who do such cannot inherit His kingdom. What a paradox! This was my situation prior to a day in November of 1993 at the University of Lagos.

The University of Lagos is located in the metropolitan city of Lagos, the commercial nerve center of Nigeria, West Africa. At the time there were more than fifteen thousand registered students attending the university—a majority of which lived on campus—with lots of activities going on at any point in time. It was so easy to be lost in the crowd, and indeed I was lost in the crowd until that particular Wednesday in November of 1993. I found myself in a Christian fellowship group for the second time and confronted with a big question: where would I spend eternity?

I was born and raised in the church. As a kid, I was taught Bible stories and also memorized Bible verses. As a teenager, I competed in sword drill (opening a given Bible passage in the shortest possible time). Most of the time, I was in the first three positions. I was well behaved, courtesy of great disciplinarians—my parents, especially my mom, who was a teacher. She never spared us the rod each time we needed it. I must confess that I did not like it at that time, but today I look back and I'm grateful for the training I received from my parents while growing up. By choice I might have gone a different way, but the love and discipline of my parents would not let me.

I grew up with strong values, which are prevalent in normal Nigerian society: values such as obeying your parents, not cursing people, and respecting those older than you. This may sound funny, but one of the ways you show respect in a typical *Yoruba* (major tribe in Nigeria) society is by prostrating yourself (if you are a male) or kneeling down (if you are a female) for elders when greeting them and by not calling people older than you by their first name. This is just one example of how I was raised.

Up until one Wednesday in November 1993, I had never given any serious thoughts to where I wanted to spend eternity. But at the end of the service that day, it dawned on me that despite my being a well-behaved gentleman, as many people often said, it was not the same as having a relationship with God. The minister on that glorious day had made an altar call for people who wanted to give their lives to Jesus so that he could pray for them. For the first time in my life, I realized the need to personally accept Christ Jesus, and I felt the conviction of the Holy Spirit asking me to step forward. I hesitated a little bit, but could not resist the redeeming power of the living God. So I went up! As I was standing in the front, I heard a voice saying to me to open my eyes and look around to see if my best friend—who was also in the meeting—came out to give his life to Christ, too. However, he was not there. A battle quickly began in me. The same voice told me my friend would be disappointed in me and suggested that if he asked me why I went forward, I should just tell him I thought everybody was and that I wasn't really serious about the commitment. Guess what happened? My friend asked me the exact question, and I answered him the way the voice had told me. I knew then that that was not the voice of God!

I have never felt as disturbed in my life as I did that night back in my room. I knew I had gone forward because I wanted to give my life to Christ—not for the reason whispered by the enemy. For two days I struggled with these thoughts, then on the third day after my encounter with the Lord, I made up my mind to go to my friend and tell him I had given my life to Christ and would not change my mind. I eventually went to his hostel and told him my decision, but what followed was unbelievable. He told me he had been thinking about giving his life to Jesus, too, for the last three days and he thought it was a good idea for us to abandon everything that did not glorify God in our lives and follow Him. This was very exciting news for me, and my joy knew no bounds. That was the beginning of my spiritual journey with the Lord.

Even though I had given my life to Christ, I was still being reminded of my sinful past as well as being lied to that my new

The Birth of a Destiny

life would be boring. It did not take too long for me to figure out that there is more to walking with the Lord than just engaging in activities. I discovered that I would need to walk with Him daily and constantly renew my strength if I was to remain in Him. This was further buttressed by the story of a Christian brother I used to know.

I will call him John. I met John several years ago when I was still just a churchgoer—simply put, when I was an unbeliever. He was very zealous for the Lord. He did house-to-house evangelism and preached to me on several occasions. His message was very clear—it is dangerous to live without Jesus. Once you die, there is no more opportunity to make it right. He often said, "Give your life to Jesus, for there is no other way by which we could be saved." It was, however, unbelievable what John was saying the next time I met him. I didn't need a Breathalyzer test to know that he was drunk, and one could easily conclude without any hesitation that he had backslidden. I was shocked! I wanted to believe I was dreaming, but I wasn't. What could have gone wrong? What could have happened? Well, the answer was not far-fetched as the Bible tells us, "Therefore let him who thinks he stands take heed that he does not fall" (1 Cor. 10:12).

We are encouraged not to be too comfortable in our current position and to seek to know God more at all times. It is difficult to find any Christian who has done so much work or suffered more pain than the apostle Paul. The Lord Jesus Christ Himself initiated his conversion. Paul heard from Christ, spoke His Word, walked in the miraculous, wrote many Bible books, was shipwrecked and jailed a number of times, and yet Paul said, "That I may know Him and the power of His resurrection" (Phil. 3:10).

As much as I was disappointed in John, I did not allow this to discourage me since I have always known that the Lord Jesus

Christ is my standard and not man. It is only by abiding in Christ that I could live a fulfilled life. Sometimes we make heroes out of pastors and church leaders and would easily go back to the world if our heroes backslide. The truth is that we are expected to make Christ our standard. He is the only perfect being that cannot disappoint, and the only source of strength and comfort that will help us grow to God's desired expectations. The Lord Jesus said, "I am the vine, you are the branches; he who abides in Me and I in him, he bears much fruit, for apart from Me you can do nothing" (John 15:5).

Sometimes as Christians we can take for granted the fact that we are human and forget that we face the same temptations and challenges that the people of the world face. Therefore, we need to be watchful and prayerful because we have an adversary in the devil whose goal is to see us fall and be separated from God.

Moses was a great vessel in the hand of God. He was called, anointed, and given a mandate by God to lead the Israelites out of bondage in Egypt into the Promised Land, yet he did not fulfill his destiny. Are you called to lead God's people as a pastor, teacher, evangelist, church worker, or music leader? Or, perhaps you are a "marketplace minister," called to establish God's kingdom in any sphere of life. No matter what your position is, you are part of the body of Christ and have been called to fulfill a specific purpose. However, you have an enemy who will seek to frustrate and destroy your destiny, just as it happened to Moses. Moses said:

> "But the LORD was angry with me on your account, and would not listen to me; and the LORD said to me, 'Enough! Speak to Me no more of this matter. *Go up to the top of Pisgah and lift up your eyes to the west and*

north and south and east, and see it with your eyes, for
you shall not cross over this Jordan.'"
—DEUTERONOMY 3:26–27, EMPHASIS ADDED

Moses prayed desperately to have his dream realized, but it was too late—his dream had been shattered. Who was Moses and how did he get to Pisgah? Come with me, and you will find out.

MOSES' BIRTH

The birth of a child is celebrated differently among the cultures of the world. Newborns are welcomed with expressions of joy and gladness by everyone around them, but that was not the case for Moses. Moses was born at a very difficult time in the life of the Israelites in Egypt, a time when Pharaoh had given an order to kill every boy who was born to the Israelites, "Then Pharaoh commanded all his people, saying, 'Every son who is born you are to cast into the Nile, and every daughter you are to keep alive'" (Exod. 1:22). Pharaoh's plan was to kill all male children, because he thought if they were allowed to live, they might grow up and fight against Egypt by joining its enemies. (See Exodus 1:8–16.) He saw women as posing no threat, but he was wrong. Can you imagine how many children were killed just to thwart the plan of God for the Israelites? The devil will do everything in his power to hinder us from fulfilling our divine destiny. The good news is that we serve a God who is able to bring to pass that which He has promised. In the case of Moses, his life was spared by divine appointment and a destiny was born. (See Exodus 2:1–10.)

When God has His hand in anything, He will leave no stone unturned in completing His will. God had His hand in the life of Moses right from the beginning. Despite Pharaoh's order, it took only four women (two Hebrew midwives, Moses' mother, and her daughter) to thwart his plan, and a deliverer was saved from the shackles of death and raised, surprisingly, in Pharaoh's own palace. Because nothing is said of the role played by Moses' father in hiding Moses, we may conclude he might have been too fearful to participate in the plot. He probably preferred his hard labor, unwilling to risk his life. But the four women were not afraid.

The same people Pharaoh thought were irrelevant were the ones the Lord used to save Moses.

> But God chose the foolish things of the world to shame the wise; God chose the weak things of the world to shame the strong. He chose the lowly things of this world and the despised things—and the things that are not—to nullify the things that are, so that no one may boast before him.
>
> —1 CORINTHIANS 1:27–29, NIV

Our God is able to use anything to bring His purpose to pass in our lives, and sometimes He uses things that we despise, ignore, or consider irrelevant. That is why He is God almighty.

For Moses' life to have been spared and even to end up living in Pharaoh's palace was nothing but a miracle only God could have performed. The Bible says Moses' mother saw that he was a very beautiful child and as a result she hid him for three months. If Moses had not been so handsome, perhaps his mother would not have hidden him. But God made Moses very attractive to the extent that his mother had no option but to go along with God's plan to save Moses.

Like Moses, we have been, "fearfully and wonderfully made" (Ps. 139:14, KJV). The living God is the only One who can turn bad situations around in our favor. "When a man's ways are pleasing to the LORD, He makes even his enemies to be at peace with him" (Prov. 16:7). When we walk in His ways and seek to please Him at all times, He will cause our enemies to live at peace with us. God has a purpose for your life just as He had a purpose for Moses' life. You are not an accident! He knew you before you were formed, because the Lord Himself said in Jeremiah 1:5, "Before I formed you in the womb I knew you, and before you were born I consecrated you; I have appointed you a prophet to the nations." It is His will that you find your purpose and receive His grace so that you may fulfill your divine destiny.

PRAYER

Heavenly Father, I thank You for the opportunity to learn from You and I give You praise. If there are any ways in which I have been taking Your grace for granted, Lord, I ask You to forgive me. Lord, as You rendered Pharaoh powerless—that he could not stop Your plan for Moses—I ask that You render powerless every power trying to abort my destiny. (See Exodus 2:9–10.) Let my ways be pleasing to You, that my enemies may live at peace with me according to Your Word in Proverbs 16:7. I also ask that You open my eyes to see what You are doing around me. Thank You for answering my prayers. In Jesus' name I pray, amen.

two

THE ESCAPE

L IVING IN LUXURY would probably be the preference of every reasonable person, especially if the alternative is living in poverty. Coming from Africa, I know what it means to be poor or go through hardship. I experienced situations where I had no money and did not know where my next meal would come from. As a result, I would usually take the opportunity to fast and pray; I had nothing to eat anyway. I also *had* to walk several miles, not for physical exercise but because I had no money for transportation. Before you start to sympathize with me, please know that there were people in worse condition than I was. At least I had a roof over my head at the time, courtesy of my brother. While I was in that situation, I kept encouraging myself that everything would be OK; the good Lord (by His Spirit) kept assuring me that it only was a passing season for me.

In contrast, Moses had lived in the palace all his life. He knew no hunger; he knew no want. Several people attended to him, and he had everything he desired. Moses must have enjoyed living in the palace—the prestige, the accolades, and the respect he got from people were enough to make him want to live in Pharaoh's palace forever, but it was a diversion and the Lord knew it.

The last job I had prior to writing this book was probably the best job I have ever had. It was a middle management position with a big organization and the prospects of moving up the management ladder were very good. I had no intention of looking for another job or working for another organization. I knew the calling of God was upon my life, but I thought I would continue to work there until the Lord made His plan plain to me.

All of a sudden, my boss started to bring up issues against me for no just reason, and it wasn't long before I realized she was trying to get me terminated. At that point I started to pray more. I also fasted and had other people praying for me. I could not entertain the thought of losing the job, but the Lord knew it was time to move forward. Just as He said to the Israelites, I had stayed long enough at that mountain. (See Deuteronomy 1:6.) God had other plans for me.

The natural tendency is for us to want to stay put in a comfortable place, and if anything threatens that, we put up a "fight." We don't want to ask God for what He thinks at that point for fear of hearing anything contrary to our own desires for comfort. The story of Joseph comes to mind. He was a man of destiny. His brothers plotted to kill him, later changed their minds, and sold him to the Midianite merchants who then took him to Egypt. Joseph was resold to Potiphar, who was one of Pharaoh's officials, the captain of the guard.

I can imagine how thankful Joseph must have been when he was put in charge of Potiphar's household. He might have thought the Lord had answered his prayers and blessed him; but what he probably did not know was that he would have to face and resist temptation, go to prison unjustly, be betrayed in prison, and then end up in charge of the whole land of Egypt. (See Genesis 37–41.) While Joseph was passing through all these phases, one thing stood out in his story—he remained faithful to the Lord his God and that was why he was able to fulfill his destiny.

So, the Lord was saying to me that I had stayed long enough at that mountain and I needed to break camp and advance to the next level. Eventually, I lost the job. About a week later, the Lord began to minister to me regarding this book. You see, I had wanted to write a book for a while, but I had no time with a full-time job. Since I was busy pursuing another degree and since I have a family (a wife and two boys who were four and two at the time), I was just too busy to listen to God. However, when I lost my job, it dawned on me that the Lord had a greater plan. He wanted my attention, He knew the job was a diversion, and He desired to fulfill His greater purpose in me.

Are you discouraged because of your current situation? Or are you so very comfortable that you are not willing to move even though the Lord is saying so? Each of us is destined for something greater than our present condition or position. Until we get to the point where the Lord wants us to be, our current situation is merely part of the process. It will not last forever and will soon pass away.

Moses' life in the palace was short-lived. Something happened one day and his life was not the same afterward. His destiny came knocking at the door of his life and he opened it.

> Now it came about in those days, when Moses had grown up, that he went out to his brethren and looked on their hard labors; and he saw an Egyptian beating a Hebrew, one of his brethren.
> —EXODUS 2:11

The Lord is waiting on us, while we are in our "Pharaoh's palace," to grow up. We will need to grow up in order to recognize that Pharaoh's palace is not God's ultimate destination for us, but just a temporary place of nurture. So when Moses had grown up, he realized his true identity and became concerned about the burdens of his people the Israelites. In an attempt to defend a fellow Israelite who was involved in a fight with an Egyptian, Moses killed the Egyptian. Moses thought nobody knew, but it had become the talk of the town and Pharaoh was seeking to kill him. (See Exodus 2:12–15.)

Many people do things in secret that they would not dare do in the presence of other people. They feel some sense of security because no one sees them. When we commit sins secretly and think no one sees us because we are good at covering up, we need to remember that the Lord sees us. Covering up seems to be the natural thing to do when we mess up, but it certainly is not the right thing. Moses thought he did a good job covering up, but his sin found him out and he was left with no option but to run.

Like Moses, sometimes we run away from God as a result of our past. Our sin might not have been murder, but it is significant enough to cost us our peace and joy. To God, sin is sin. It is disobedience to His Word. There is no small sin or big sin. The good news is, "If we confess our sins, he is faithful and just to forgive us our sins, and to cleanse us from all unrighteousness" (1 John 1:9, KJV). Instead of covering up, we can quickly take advantage of the Lord's offer.

Moses tried to find peace elsewhere, but the Lord who is faithful and loving was not done with him yet. He had a plan and purpose for his life, so He sought him in his hiding place. When we hide from the shame of our past, the Lord is calling us to come out of our hiding place so that we can fulfill His purpose for our life. He is a gracious God. He did it in the life of Moses, and He wants to do the same in our life. Knowing the Lord's purpose is not enough, however; we need to be equipped by Him to be prepared to fulfill that purpose.

PRAYER

My Father and my God, I thank You for the revelation of Your Word to me. I confess every secret sin in my life, and I ask for forgiveness. Lord, I ask that You remove every distraction placed in my way to fulfilling Your divine destiny for my life. Lord, according to Your Word, I shall not die, but live, and declare the works of the Lord (see Psalm 118:17, KJV). I also pray that when my destiny comes knocking at the door of my life, I shall open the door. In Jesus' glorious name I pray, amen.

three

ENCOUNTER WITH GOD

T HE OLD SAYING, "Ignorance is a disease," is very true. Ignorance would rob anyone of readily available blessings if he or she is not aware of such blessings. I remember my first encounter with an automatic faucet. My wife and I were coming to the US and had a stopover at Boston's Airport. I went to use the bathroom and needed to wash my hands. I stood in front of the sink helpless, as there was no handle on the faucet. I moved to the other sinks, but they all looked the same. As I stood there in awe, a gentleman stepped up to wash his hands. I pretended to be looking at the mirror, but in fact I was watching him to see how he would operate the water faucet. He just stretched forth his hands beneath the faucet and water began to flow. I quickly did the same thing and water poured out on my hands. What a relief!

I was in a similar state of ignorance when a family friend said I should pray that God would bring me my future spouse. The friend said that a child of God must not be unequally yoked with an unbeliever, referring to 2 Corinthians 6:14. I had not had a personal encounter with Christ, so I made fun of her and told her how stupid the idea was—to absolutely rely on God to reveal and give one a future spouse. I specifically remember asking her, "What if God revealed an ugly person?" She tried to explain, but my mind was made up and I was not ready to give it any thought. What I did not know was that even though I professed to believe in God, I had sealed my heart against certain truths in His Word. However, once I gave my life to the Lord in November 1993, I made a decision to trust Him for everything, even for a wife. Only then was I able to comprehend the Word of God properly, fulfilling 1 Corinthians 2:14 (NIV):

> The man without the Spirit does not accept the things that come from the Spirit of God, for they are foolishness to him, and he cannot understand them, because they are spiritually discerned.

My eyes were newly opened and my heart was receptive because the Spirit of God was living in me. I had had an encounter with God.

An encounter with God is an unforgettable experience. It has the power to change the course of one's life forever. An encounter with God is something to desire, thirst for, and seek after. Jacob had an encounter with God and had his name changed to Israel in Genesis 32:22–28. Jabez called on the God of Israel and he became more honorable than his brothers in 1 Chronicles 4:9–10. The woman with an issue of blood had an encounter with the Lord Jesus and her blood flow ceased in Luke 8:43–44. Blind Bartimaeus had an encounter with the Lord Jesus and had his sight restored in Mark 10:46–52. Moses also had an encounter with God and the course of his life was changed. You cannot have an encounter with God and remain the same. It is just not possible!

At that time Moses was living as an alien in a foreign land. He was married and had a child. At that juncture in his life, Moses must have accepted his fate. Of course he was not thinking of going back to his people in Egypt, but the Lord who had a purpose for his life had not forgotten. God's gifts and call upon His children are irrevocable. (See Romans 11:29.)

One great example of the irrevocable call of God on one's life is the case of Jonah. Jonah was called by the Lord to go to the city of Nineveh and preach against it because of its wickedness. Instead, Jonah fled from the Lord and headed for Tarshish. It took three days and three nights inside a great fish before Jonah came to his senses, prayed to the Lord his God, and accepted the call of God for his life. (See Jonah 1–2.)

You cannot outrun God. If He has called you for a specific purpose, He will not change His mind. Like Jonah, Moses might have fled from Egypt (his appointed place with destiny), but the Lord would not change His mind regarding His call upon him. One day while Moses was tending the flock of Jethro, his father-in-law, the Lord appeared to him and said:

> And now the cry of the Israelites has reached me, and I have seen the way the Egyptians are oppressing them. So now, go. I am sending you to Pharaoh to bring my people the Israelites out of Egypt.
>
> —EXODUS 3:9–10, NIV

We serve a compassionate God who hears our prayers when we call upon Him. He empathizes with us even in difficult situations and cannot ignore our cry. He heard the cry of the Israelites, but He needed a contact person, someone to send to Pharaoh and bring the Israelites out of Egypt. Thus He planned to send Moses. However, Moses' past quickly came haunting him. The thought of going on trial for murder if he should go back to Egypt probably crossed his mind. This was evident in his response to God, "But Moses said to God, 'Who am I, that I should go to Pharaoh and bring the Israelites out of Egypt?'" (Exod. 3:11, NIV).

Like Moses, many of God's children often look at their inabilities when He calls. We allow our past to dictate how far we want to go with God, forgetting that it is not about us but about Him. What the Lord is saying to us is the same thing He said to apostle Paul in 2 Corinthians 12:9, "My grace is sufficient for you, for my power is made perfect in weakness" (NIV). The task may be daunting, and you may feel too weak to get the job done, but the truth of the matter is that on your own you cannot do it. But by His grace and His power you can do all things. Our God is a forgiving, merciful, kind, and gracious God. He forgives and forgets our past if only we will repent and forsake our old ways.

The Lord's response to Moses' excuse was filled with grace. He said, "Certainly I will be with you, and this shall be the sign to you that it is I who have sent you: when you have brought the people out of Egypt, you shall worship God at this mountain" (Exod. 3:12). The Lord not only promised to be with Moses, but also gave signs because He knew what was going on in Moses' mind. Despite this assurance, Moses put up further resistance. "Moses said to God, 'Suppose I go to the Israelites and say to them, "The God of your fathers has sent me to you," and they ask me, "What is his name?" Then what shall I tell them?'" (Exod. 3:13, NIV). We might naturally condemn Moses for going this far, but everyone in Egypt would have known what he had done. The implication was that he had no reputation, and if he did it was a very bad one. What would we have done? Moses was probably wondering how someone like him could be given such a great task, and he wanted to make sure he was hearing right. The Lord, who is slow to anger, answered him, "I AM WHO I AM," and, "Thus you shall say to the sons of Israel, 'I AM has sent me to you'" (Exod. 3:14). The Lord then instructed Moses on what to do and gave further insight into what he would do in Egypt.

It is obvious: the Lord does not give up on us. He will do everything in His power to bring to fruition that which He has ordained. That is why He keeps coming to us in spite of our not doing what we perceive He wants us to do. Even though Moses did not know the scope of his calling, his life would be transformed as a result of his encounter with God.

You are a miracle in the making, too. We do not need to be concerned about our past. We are a new creation in Christ; old things have passed away, and all things have become new. (See 2 Corinthians 5:17.) The Lord has forgiven and forgotten our past mistakes. You may not know how God intends to bring His purpose to fulfillment in your life, but rest assured, He will not let you down. If He has called you, He will empower you.

Prayer

I thank You, King of kings and Lord of lords, for this precious moment in my life. I also thank You for not giving up on me. I release myself in the name of Jesus from every activity of the past that has held me captive. According to 2 Timothy 1:7, I refuse to be afraid of the future, but instead I look up to You who are able to do all things. I also receive power from You to do that which You have called me to, in Jesus' name, amen.

four

MORE EXCUSES

W E ONLY OFFER excuses for things we don't have any interest in. We simply try to offer an explanation with the hope that the other party will understand and let it go. I learned a great lesson about excuses and accountability through the life of a Christian brother in my church in Nigeria.

By Nigeria's standard, David is well-to-do. I went with him in his car one day to visit another brother who was sick and had been admitted to one of the general hospitals in Lagos. We were trying to locate the sick brother, when we noticed a small crowd gathered around a teenage boy who had a blood-soaked bandage around his foot and ankle. A woman who happened to be the boy's mother was crying uncontrollably, so we approached them. As we got closer, we knew it was a bad situation as there was blood everywhere on the ground where the boy was sitting.

"What happened?" we asked.

The mother explained that the boy, a roadside food hawker (vendor) was run over by a hit-and-run driver on a very busy road in Lagos. Lagos has a lot of roadside hawkers who sell things to motorists in slow-moving traffic. While there are lots of fatalities with this type of solicitation, these hawkers do not think twice about the kind of risks they take out of desperation for survival. David asked why the boy had not been attended to and the mother said they were told the boy urgently needed a blood transfusion, but would not be attended to without paying the cost of the procedure in advance. Since they could not afford the cost and had no means of stopping the blood loss, their only option was to sit outside the ward sobbing with the hope that someone would have mercy on them.

The boy was passing in and out of consciousness as he continued to lose blood. Unfortunately, neither David nor I had the money to help these people right away. We therefore had an excuse not to get involved, but David would not give up. He approached one of the doctors, introduced himself, and requested that the boy be attended to with a promise to pay up his bill the following day. The doctor said he would not be able to help without a concrete guarantee that he would be back the following day to pay the boy's bill. According to the doctor, he had tried to help people in similar situations only to end up paying their bills when they defaulted. He explained further that the hospital policy was to automatically deduct from the guarantor's salary if he or she was a staff member. At that point, David removed his gold wedding ring and gave it to the doctor just to assure him he would be back the following day to pay up the bill. When we got there the following day, the boy had been taken care of. His mother could not thank my friend enough for saving her son's life.

Most of the time we give excuses to escape responsibility. The reason we do this is that we are concerned about ourselves. We fear for our lives and consider other people secondary. However, giving God excuses never works, because He sees into our hearts and knows our abilities. He would rather have us come out straight and tell Him we are afraid and need His help. It is better to tell Him we are intimidated by the task and need His assurance, rather than to try to justify our disobedience to His commands. God knew Moses was not being plain with Him, and He surely knows the motives for our actions, too.

"Moses answered, 'But behold, they will not believe me or listen to my voice, for they will say, "The LORD did not appear to you"'" (Exod. 4:1 NIV). How frustrating! Moses was preempting God. He was acting as if he were a god in God's presence by telling God what would happen. Moses might have forgotten that he was standing before the God who is Alpha and Omega, the Beginning and the End. (See Revelation 21:6.) But we also do that: we tell God what we perceive will happen even when He is telling us the contrary. But God is ever faithful. He loves us much more than we can ever imagine.

God was not discouraged with Moses' attitude because He saw in him a great vessel that He could use. God responded to Moses' now familiar excuses with several signs just to assure him. (See Exodus 4:2–9.) One would think that after all those signs Moses would gladly accept the call of God for his life. Well, he didn't. Moses was still not convinced that the Lord would go with him. Perhaps he was still afraid of the consequences of his past and was thinking of what would be done to him once he got to Egypt. We must surrender our past to God and give Him a free hand to turn it around for His glory. Moses' excuse was not acceptable anyway, because his motive contradicted the Word of God. The Bible says, "For God has not given us a spirit of timidity, but of power and love and discipline" (2 Tim. 1:7).

Fear is not of God but of the devil. The only fear God's children are expected to have is the fear of the living God, "The fear of the LORD is the beginning of wisdom, and the knowledge of the Holy One is understanding" (Prov. 9:10). When we fear God, we will have wisdom and we will gain insight into His will. The fear of man is probably one of the biggest problems confronting us as Christians today. We are afraid of what peoples' reactions will be or what they will say to us when God prompts us to share the good news with them. We will start to rationalize and give God excuses as to why we are not able to do what He wants us to do, just as Moses did. Sometimes we are too ashamed to stand for God, forgetting that the most popular name in heaven and on earth is *Jesus*. Each time we refuse to stand for God, what we are doing is embracing the spirit of fear, which is of the devil, and rejecting the Spirit of God, who gives boldness.

So Moses came up with yet another excuse. "Then Moses said to the LORD, 'Please, Lord, I have never been eloquent, neither recently nor in time past, nor since You have spoken to Your servant; for I am slow of speech and slow of tongue'" (Exod. 4:10). That was Moses' complaint number four. Unbelievable! At that juncture, it was obvious that Moses had a complaining problem. What else could God have done to make him go? If you or I were God, we would probably have written Moses off at this point, but our God who is slow to anger was willing to give him another opportunity:

> The LORD said to him, "Who has made man's mouth? Or who makes him mute or deaf, or seeing or blind? Is it not I, the LORD? Now then go, and I, even I, will be with your mouth, and teach you what you are to say."
> —EXODUS 4:11–12

What a gracious God we serve! "The LORD is compassionate and gracious, Slow to anger and abounding in lovingkindness." (Ps. 103:8).

Moses was not done with God yet, though. He had talked to God about his so-called concerns, but he was just trying to find a way out of God's plan for his life. Having tried everything else, but to no avail, he then finally came out to declare his hidden agenda, "But Moses said, 'O Lord, please send someone else to do it'" (Exod. 4:13, NIV). This was the straw that broke the camel's back.

> Then the anger of the LORD burned against Moses, and He said, "Is there not your brother Aaron the Levite? I know that he speaks fluently. And moreover, behold, he is coming out to meet you; when he sees you, he will be glad in his heart. You are to speak to him and put the words in his mouth; and I, even I, will be with your mouth and his mouth, and I will teach you what you are to do. Moreover, he shall speak for you to the people; and he will be as a mouth for you and you will be as God to him."
>
> —EXODUS 4:14–16

The Lord could no longer deal with Moses' excuses, yet He was unwilling to change His mind regarding sending Moses to Pharaoh. So He did what He probably didn't plan to do—He provided Aaron, Moses' brother, to accompany him and be his mouthpiece. It was obvious that God originally meant for Moses to go alone to Egypt, but his persistent complaints led him to God's permissive will, and thus unnoticed, his journey to Pisgah began.

It is important that we seek the mind of God regarding any issue in our lives. It will save us a lot of trouble. It is by abiding in the will of God that we can have His peace and fulfill His divine destiny for our lives.

PRAYER

Heavenly Father, I thank You because You always give a second chance. I am so grateful for being counted worthy to be used of You. I pray that henceforth I shall no longer be a barrier to Your plan for my life. I ask that You give me Your discerning Spirit that I may recognize Your will for my life and receive the power to cooperate with Your plan for my life from now on. I pray in Jesus' name, amen.

five

MOSES THE INTERCESSOR

INTERCESSION IS PRAYING to God on behalf of other people. Moses was a master at intercession. While many of us are used to asking in prayers just for ourselves, intercessors are more concerned about the affairs of others. The Lord taught me a lesson on intercession a while ago.

At that time my older brother was still a nonbeliever. I was living with him because I could not afford my own accommodation. As a new believer, I despised all his sinful ways—drinking, partying, and going out with all kinds of women. I would pick on him over anything I perceived was not right, until one day he said, "You can behave like a saint now, but you also used to do some of these things." Immediately as he said that, the Lord told me that it was true. The Lord said I was once a sinner before I found mercy and that if I was not pleased with my brother's lifestyle, I should pray for him rather than condemn him. That got me! I felt ashamed about my attitude toward my brother and made up my mind to intercede for him from that point on.

My parents and other siblings prayed for him continually, and he eventually gave his life to the Lord. He is so strong in the Lord now and often fasts for several days at a time, even up to seventy days. God is awesome! A holier-than-thou attitude will not do us any good; instead it will encourage sinners to keep on sinning. I also learned after my older brother's conversion that my little brother had interceded for me, fasting for seven days when I was an unbeliever. I tell you God is still in the business of changing hearts, and if intercessors will step up their petition to God, we can be sure of great results.

Moses was not an ordinary person, and I'm sure the Lord knew that. He might have had problems accepting the call of God initially, but he lived a transformed life afterward. One of Moses' attributes was intercession. He was certainly one of the greatest intercessors who ever lived, and you are about to see this for yourself. Exodus 5:22–23 reads:

> Then Moses returned to the LORD and said, "O Lord, why have You brought harm to this people? Why did You ever send me? Ever since I came to Pharaoh to speak in Your name, he has done harm to this people, and You have not delivered Your people at all."

Moses had gone to God because Pharaoh compounded the task of the Israelites. Instead of providing straw, which the Israelites needed to make bricks, as was the usual practice prior to Moses' return to Egypt, they were now required to gather their own straw and still meet their daily quota of bricks. The Israelites did not take this very kindly. They became very angry with him and were calling for his head, but Moses, rather than getting into an argument with them, went back to the Lord and cried out to Him on behalf of the people. Although Moses also expressed his disappointment with God here, which was uncalled for, he subsequently perfected the art of intercession without any ulterior motive.

AT MARAH

After Pharaoh and his army had been drowned in the Red Sea, the Israelites traveled three days in the desert without water. They got to Marah, and the water there was bitter. As would be expected, the people grumbled against Moses again. Moses then cried to the Lord and the Lord showed him a tree and he threw it into the water and the water became sweet. (See Exodus 15:24–25.) Moses cried out to God on behalf of the people again and the Lord answered him. Not only did the Lord answer him, He also made a vow not to spare them of the diseases He put on Egypt. Spiritually, Egypt represents the world, a state of being out of the will of God, worldliness. Its diseases are discomfort, sorrow, lack, unprecedented loss, confusion, famine, and so on. God gave four keys to avoiding these situations in Exodus 15:26 and these are:

1. Diligently hearken to the voice of the Lord

According to the *Webster's Dictionary*, to be *diligent* is to "quietly and steadily persevere especially in detail or exactness." Our God is a very detailed God. He wants to give us instructions, but there is no way we are going to hear Him if we are distracted; and there is no way we can please Him if we do not do as He instructs. God speaks in different ways to His children. He speaks through the Bible, an audible voice, inner witness, circumstances, and prayers. God is calling us to listen attentively to His voice, as this is the only way His Word can benefit us.

2. Do that which is right in His eyes

God has given everyone a conscience. It is generally believed that our conscience is what guides and encourages us to make the right decision especially when faced with a right or wrong situation. To a Christian, the Holy Spirit is the One in charge of our conscience, and He helps us to make not just the right decisions but also godly decisions. It is however unfortunate that sometimes we still prefer to do the wrong things. It doesn't bother some people when they make wrong choices because they believe God is merciful. Well, that is taking God's grace for granted: "Therefore, to one who knows the right thing to do and does not do it, to him it is sin" (James 4:17). What God is saying to us here is to run away from sin. Study the Bible and do what it says, pray and fellowship, and we can be sure the Holy Spirit will be with us always, and with Him we cannot go wrong.

3. Heed His commandments

The Lord is saying we should pay attention to His commandments, "Thy word have I hid in mine heart, that I might not sin against thee" (Ps. 119:11, KJV). When we pay attention to the Lord's commandments, it will be difficult for us to go against them. In other words, we will live in obedience and His blessings will always abound to us.

4. Keep His statutes

Not only are we expected to obey His commandments, but we are also expected to keep His decrees, and there are several of them in the Bible.

> These are the things that ye shall do; Speak ye every man the truth to his neighbour; execute the judgment of truth and peace in your gates: And let none of you imagine evil in your hearts against his neighbor; and love no false oath: for all these are things that I hate, saith the LORD."
>
> —ZECHARIAH 8:16–17, KJV

It is therefore expedient that we meditate upon His Word at all times.

If we will do all four of these things, we will be bound to enjoy the favor of the Lord all the days of our lives. Oppression will be far from us, and the rod of the wicked shall not fall upon our lot because we are the Lord's righteous. (See Psalm 125:3, KJV.)

Now let's go back to Moses the intercessor.

AT MOUNT SINAI

> Now when the people saw that Moses delayed to come down from the mountain, the people assembled about Aaron and said to him, "Come, make us a god who will go before us; as for this Moses, the man who brought us up from the land of Egypt, we do not know what has become of him."
>
> —EXODUS 32:1

It was obvious Moses had a daunting task leading the Israelites. Their attitudes were very contrary to God's expectation of them, in spite of all the great miracles He had done in their midst. They were rebellious and unstable in their walk with God. They requested for a man-made god, an idol that they could see and worship, and God was displeased with them. God was ready to destroy them because of their stubbornness, and made a promise to make Moses into a great nation upon the destruction of the people. (See Exodus 32:9–10.)

How many people could resist this offer from God? Well, Moses did. Many of us would not hesitate to accept this type of offer. We have seen people in high places taking advantage of their subjects. They have more wealth than their subjects by exploiting them and are still seeking to have more. It is unfortunate that this type of greed has even crawled into the church. It is my prayer that the Lord will give us the wisdom to do His will at all times. All that Moses needed was to agree with the Lord's proposal and He would have made him into a great nation, yet he refused. Moses did not want to be blessed at the expense of the Israelites. What an incredible, thoughtful, and unselfish leader Moses was!

Moses' response to God was extraordinary:

> Then Moses entreated the LORD his God, and said, "O LORD, why does Your anger burn against Your people whom You have brought out from the land of Egypt with great power and with a mighty hand? Why should the Egyptians speak, saying, 'With evil intent He brought them out to kill them in the mountains and to destroy them from the face of the earth?' Turn from Your burning anger and change Your mind about doing harm to Your people. Remember Abraham, Isaac, and Israel, Your servants to whom You swore by Yourself, and said to them, 'I will multiply your descendants as the stars of the heavens, and all this land of which I have spoken I will give to your descendants, and they shall inherit it forever.'"
> —EXODUS 32:11–13

Moses interceded earnestly for the people. He pleaded with God on behalf of the people and reminded God of the implication of His planned action. He also reminded God of His earlier promises, and made a case with God to change His mind. What was the result? "So the LORD changed His mind about the harm which He said He would do to His people" (Exod. 32:14).

If you think that was all the intercession Moses did, then you need to read on.

AT TABERAH

The Israelites once again complained about their misfortunes and the Lord was not pleased. He became angry with them and He sent fire to consume them. (See Numbers 11:1.) The natural thing we want to do when we are not pleased about a situation is to complain. In the worldly political system this is probably the right thing to do, especially if we want the attention of the authority that is in place. Often they will listen to our complaints, and if many people are involved, they may even be forced to change their mind on the issue. However, in kingdom business, complaining is not necessary since we have access to the throne of God. Our God is unlike the worldly kings. He orders our steps, He knows our needs, He sees our suffering, He never loses track of our situation, and He cannot be late. Whatever He does is for our good. The people had gotten it wrong again, but they cried out to God and Moses' intercession stopped the fire of the Lord from consuming them all. (See Numbers 11:2–3.)

MIRIAM AND AARON

Miriam and Aaron criticized Moses because of his Cushite wife, and the Lord was not happy about it. (See Numbers 12:1–2.) When you speak against God's anointed, you are literally speaking against God and the result can be disastrous. In the case of Miriam and Aaron, they got more than they bargained for. The Lord's anger burned against them:

> But when the cloud had withdrawn from over the tent, behold, Miriam was leprous, as white as snow. As Aaron turned toward Miriam, behold, she was leprous. Then Aaron said to Moses: "Oh, my lord, I beg you, do not account this sin to us, in which we have acted foolishly and in which we have sinned. Oh, do not let her be like one dead, whose flesh is half eaten away when he comes from his mother's womb!"
> —NUMBERS 12:10–12

One would think this would make Moses happy—at least the Lord had dealt with his accusers. Not so! "And Moses cried unto the LORD, saying, Heal her now, O God, I beseech thee" (Num. 12:13, KJV). The result? The Lord answered Moses' prayer and healed Miriam.

AT THE DESERT OF PARAN

Moses had carried out the Lord's instruction to send men to explore Canaan. Twelve men representing each tribe were sent. Two of the twelve, Caleb and Joshua, came back with a favorable report, but the remaining ten men came back with a fearful report that sent jitters down the spines of the Israelites. As usual the people became afraid and rebelled because of the bad report. They believed the lie of the enemy instead of the report of the Lord. Whose report are we going to believe? Situations around us may be very intimidating, but the good news is that if we have given our lives to Jesus, He is able to take care of us and our situations.

The Israelites succumbed to fear and even contemplated stoning Moses and Aaron. The Lord's anger burned again, and He was prepared to strike them down with a plague and destroy them. Again, the Lord promised to make Moses into a great nation, even greater than the people. Again, Moses rejected God's offer and cried out on behalf of the people. (See Numbers 14:13–19.) Moses knew how to approach God. He knew the Lord is faithful and would always honor His Word. So what did he do this time? He reminded God of His Word, targeting His promises and attributes, and the Lord once again changed His mind. "So the LORD said, 'I have pardoned them according to your word'" (Num. 14:20).

The Lord honors His words even above His name. He will always pardon when we pray according to His Word and His promises. We desperately need intercessors today, people who will ignore their personal benefits for the sake of the perishing; intercessors who are unselfish, heaven conscious, and who would do everything possible to stop destruction from coming upon the sinners. However, if we are to intercede successfully, we will need to have a one-on-one relationship with the Lord. We must know His Word and His attributes, then, just like Moses, we will always move the hand of God. It is my prayer that you will consider being an intercessor.

PRAYER

Heavenly Lord, I thank You for Your compassion and love. I thank You for listening to me when I call upon You. Thank You for making me a partaker of Your divine nature, as it tells me in 2 Peter 1:4. Lord, I ask this day that You give me a compassionate heart that I may intercede on behalf of those who are lost. Let me not put my hands into iniquity that I may be a vessel of honor in Your hands. Let me radiate Your true love from now on. In Jesus' name I pray, amen.

six

GOD DELIGHTS IN THE HUMBLE

H UMILITY IS NOT being weak or foolish. It is recognizing the lordship of our Savior Jesus Christ over our life, and giving in to the leadership of the Holy Spirit, such that whatever He says, we will do.

There was a story of a Christian brother who was slapped by an unbeliever who cited Matthew 5:39 as his reason for slapping him. Matthew 5:39 says, "But I say to you, Do not resist one who is evil. But if any one strikes you on the right cheek, turn to him the other also." The Christian brother then turned his left cheek also, and the unbeliever slapped him the second time. When the Christian brother was asked why he did that, his answer was that Christ wanted us to be humble. That was not humility, neither was that suffering for Christ. That was simply not applying wisdom. Common sense demands that you don't put yourself in a situation where someone can twist the meaning of God's Word to suit his or her purpose. It was like the devil trying to tempt the Lord Jesus Christ by misquoting the Bible. Well, Jesus reminded him of the written Word of God rather than giving into temptation.

Humility is reverencing God in every aspect of your life. Moses was a very humble man. God said of Moses in Numbers 12:3, "Now the man Moses was very humble, more than any man who was on the face of the earth." Have you ever wondered why the Lord chose Moses and showed him much favor each time he interceded? Well, the Lord made it clear that

His dwelling place is high and holy. God dwells with him who is of a contrite and humble spirit. (See Isaiah 57:15, KJV.) If we would be His dwelling place, then we must detest pride and put on His garment of humility. Humility is an attribute that every Christian should have, especially since we are named after Christ. The Bible says of the Lord Jesus Christ, "And being found in fashion as a man, he humbled himself, and became obedient unto death, even the death of the cross" (Phil. 2:8, KJV). The Lord Jesus had the power to destroy His adversaries. He had the power to prevent His crucifixion because He was God in human form. Yet, He humbled himself and was killed in a gruesome manner. It is clear that the Lord's humility was the key to fulfilling His purpose on earth. He was God, yet He became man. He suffered pain, He was hungry, thirsty, and tempted while on earth, and He went through all these that He might work out the salvation of man.

CONSEQUENCES OF HUMILITY

Grace

The grace of God is often described as God's undeserved mercy. It was obvious Moses enjoyed the Lord's undeserved mercy to the end of his assignment. The Lord's grace is available to every humble child of His. "But He gives a greater grace. Therefore it says, 'GOD IS OPPOSED TO THE PROUD, BUT GIVES GRACE TO THE HUMBLE'" (James 4:6). We need God's grace in order to be successful in this Christian race. I challenge you this moment to humble yourself and you will begin to enjoy more of His grace.

Lifting

"Humble yourselves in the presence of the Lord, and He will exalt you" (James 4:10). To lift is to exalt and according to the dictionary, to *exalt* is to "raise in rank, character, or status; also to elevate." It is not appropriate for a Christian to struggle for everything in life just as the unbelievers do, especially because we serve a God who is the only One who can truly promote and bless.

> "I say to the boastful, 'Do not boast,' And to the wicked, 'Do not lift up your horn; Do not lift up your horn on high, Do not speak with insolent pride.'" For not from the east, nor from the west, Nor from the desert comes exaltation; But God is the judge; He puts down one and exalts another.
>
> —PSALM 75:4–7

The living God is the only one who can lift us up. He is also the Giver of good gifts. (See Matthew 7:11; Luke 11:13.) Are you looking for a lifting in your marriage, career, finances, and all your endeavors? You will need to humble yourself—and rest assured that when He exalts you, no man could pull you down.

Forgiveness

Forgiving other people when they hurt us is probably the most difficult thing to do, but it is often the key to unlocking God's abundant joy, peace, and stress-free living into our lives. I found out how easy it is to harbor an unforgiving spirit even as a Christian. I had worked with this company for about two years in two different capacities, and had given my best to the job. My supervisor in the previous position called me an asset to the company. When I lost the job, I found it difficult to understand why someone would be interested in taking my job for no just reason. I felt bad, but took solace in the fact that the Lord is in charge and that He had allowed it because He wanted to move me up. However, deep down in my heart I was hurt and expected the Lord to repay my former boss in the same coin as I was paid. But one day, I was on the freeway driving home from town when the Lord told me to pray for my boss who had hurt me. My initial feeling was that of disappointment. Does that mean the Lord would not punish the wickedness that was done to me? It dawned on me that there was some bitterness in me and I needed to deal with it. I remembered that I have been forgiven much by the Lord and needed to let go. While still driving I began to pray for my boss and everyone I had worked with. Tears began to roll down my cheeks and the joy that I felt afterward was indescribable.

God expects us to forgive others when they hurt us and to ask for forgiveness when we hurt others. One of the requirements we need to satisfy in order to obtain forgiveness is humility. Humility always leads to reconciliation with God. The Bible says in 2 Chronicles 7:14 (NIV):

> If my people, who are called by my name, will humble themselves and pray and seek my face and turn from their wicked ways, then will I hear from heaven and will forgive their sin and will heal their land.

Humility brings about genuine repentance. No matter what we might have done, if we will humble ourselves before God, pray, seek His face, and turn from our wicked ways, then God will do His part. He will hear from heaven, forgive our sin, and heal our land. Amen.

Answered Prayer

During Josiah's reign as king of Judah, the book of the law was found in the temple of the Lord and read in the hearing of the king, and the king reacted spontaneously to the word that he heard. That tells me how powerful the Word of the Lord is. The Word of the Lord is very powerful and can produce tremendous changes in our lives. The Word reveals our state of mind, convicts us of sins, and sets us free. This was what King Josiah experienced after hearing the Word of the Lord, "When the king heard the words of the book of the law, he tore his clothes" (2 Kings 22:11). King Josiah was very concerned about what the Word of God said. He then gave orders to his officials to go and inquire of the Lord about what was written. The Lord said through prophetess Huldah, that His anger would not be quenched and that He would fulfill all that was written:

> "But to the king of Judah who sent you to inquire of the Lord thus shall you say to him, 'Thus says the Lord God of Israel, "Regarding the words which you have heard, because your heart was tender and *you humbled yourself before the Lord* when you heard what I spoke against this place and against its inhabitants that they should become a desolation and a curse, and you have torn your clothes and wept before Me, I truly have heard you," declares the Lord. "Therefore, behold, I will gather you to your fathers, and you will be gathered to your grave in peace, and your eyes will not see all the evil which I will bring on this place"'"
> —2 Kings 22:18–20, emphasis added

King Josiah's humility caught God's attention and his prayer was answered. If we will humble ourselves, we will have our prayers answered even in the face of pending destruction.

Deliverance

The dictionary meaning of *deliverance* is "rescued from bondage or danger." You get in bondage when you lose your God-given authority to something else, and you become subject to its control. This can be physical or spiritual.

Being in danger is a terrifying experience and no one, no matter how bold, can look forward to such an experience. I remember my friend's encounter with the men of the underworld. At the time he was living with his older brother who was a bank executive. They were already sleeping when suddenly they were awakened in the middle of the night by sounds of gunshots in their compound. They immediately knew that armed robbers had invaded their property. Everyone in the house started to run helter-skelter and the robbers came into their house. The robbers asked him, his brother, and his sister in-law to lie down in the living room and demanded money and jewelry, but his brother did not have much cash at home. The robbers knew his brother was a bank executive and threatened to kill him if he didn't come up with the amount demanded in a few minutes.

My friend could not describe the panic and fear that enveloped him when he heard his brother begging for his life. His brother got so confused that he told the armed robber he would go to the bank the following day to withdraw money for them if they would spare his life. My friend groaned before God to save them and eventually the armed robbers went away after taking all the valuables in the house. What my friend, his brother, and his sister in-law experienced was a great deliverance from the Lord in the midst of danger.

King Rehoboam and the princes of Israel were also in danger of pending destruction because they forsook the law of the Lord.

> Then Shemaiah the prophet came to Rehoboam and the princes of Judah who had gathered at Jerusalem because of Shishak, and he said to them, "Thus says the LORD, You have forsaken Me, so I also have forsaken you to Shishak." So the *princes of Israel and the king*

humbled themselves and said, "The LORD is righteous." When the LORD saw that they humbled themselves, the word of the LORD came to Shemaiah, saying, "They have humbled themselves so I will not destroy them, but I will grant them some measure of deliverance, and My wrath shall not be poured out on Jerusalem by means of Shishak."

—2 CHRONICLES 12:5–7, EMPHASIS ADDED

Humility always leads to deliverance. Israel, its leaders, and the king were about to be destroyed. They humbled themselves before God, and the Lord delivered them.

Moses' humility was comparable to none, and that was one of the reasons he had so much favor with God. Humility before God will always grant us great deliverance and unimaginable breakthroughs.

PRAYER

My Father and my God, I thank You once again for revealing Yourself to me. Thank You for humbling Yourself and becoming obedient unto death, even death on a cross, just for my sake. I renounce and reject every spirit of pride in me from now on. By the anointing of the Holy Spirit, let the yoke of bitterness be broken in my life. I receive the grace to forgive all those who have hurt me in the past. Lord Jesus, I ask that You put Your humble Spirit in me henceforth. In Your mighty name I pray, amen.

seven

MOSES THE WATCHMAN

THE ISRAELITES HAD proven to be a very difficult people to lead. Moses seemed to be aware of this and I believe he was prepared to go the extra mile with them, especially considering the way he interceded for them. Moses stood in the gap for the people each time they sinned against God. He was a watchman to the core. The Book of Ezekiel 33:1–7 gives an account of the Lord's expectations of a watchman. According to the passage, a watchman needs to blow the trumpet and warn the people of whatever he hears from the mouth of the Lord.

A watchman is the one who keeps watch. He sits on a tower, which gives him an advantage to see objects around him clearly. When a potential enemy is approaching the camp, he will be the one to see it first and alert the people. I believe that a watchman must not be suffering from farsightedness (a term for an abnormal condition in which one is able to see distant objects better that near objects), or nearsightedness (a term for an abnormal condition in which one is able to see near objects better that distant objects). He must have perfect vision and be able to see what God is doing around him. A watchman must also be a good listener so that when God speaks, he will hear clearly and warn the people appropriately of the looming danger and destruction awaiting them if they refuse to listen to the Lord's command. Moses heard the word of God clearly, saw what God was doing, and warned the people appropriately. He was a good example of what leadership is all about.

I had first hand experience of what it means to be a watchman in the year 1995. At that time I was still a member of the National Youth Service Corps (NYSC), a government agency made up of fresh graduates from universities and colleges in Nigeria. In Nigeria, there is a one-year government mandated service that graduates must observe before seeking gainful employment. During this period I was a member of the Nigerian Christian Corpers' Fellowship (NCCF). The NCCF mission is to spread the gospel of our Lord Jesus Christ.

Several crusades were organized in little villages where idol worship was the order of the day. On many occasions, those idol worshippers threatened the Christian fellowship in order to prevent us from coming to their community. There was a particular incident when the leaders of one of the communities filed a complaint with the government agency. All their idols had stopped communicating with them after a visit to the town by the Christian Fellowship.

Please note that we just didn't go to these places by chance. The first thing the Christian fellowship did was to send its prayer secretary to a community that it intended to visit. At the community, the prayer secretary would research their beliefs, their problems, and other prayer needs deemed necessary, usually with the help of a Christian resident in the community. Dates of the intended crusades would be fixed and publicity would begin. A three-day fasting and prayer would then be organized to pray for the village or town we intended to visit. We would then go ahead with the crusades at the village, and usually we would come back with outstanding testimonies.

This particular occasion, we went to a village regardless of the now familiar threats to prevent us from coming. The village was known for its idol worship and evil altars. We were told that a missionary had died mysteriously due to his non-compliance with a restriction not to preach in a place declared out of bounds to Christians. One noticeable feature in many of these communities where idol worship is still prevalent is the lack of meaningful development. This particular village like the others lacked basic infrastructures—no electricity or pipe-borne water.

We slept in the classrooms of the village elementary school, which had dilapidated walls and missing windows and doors. It started to rain the first day of the three-day crusade, and continued to rain throughout the entire program. We took a step further to beat the enemy at his game. We set up a security force of watchmen, which were rotated every hour or two during the night. Their job included watching the perimeter of the building where we slept, praying while watching, and alerting the remaining group of any threat to our safety. While on duty you could not afford to take a nap or be careless. You constantly had to be praying as the intensity of the power of darkness could be felt all around.

To the glory of God, the Lord protected us throughout the three days and the villagers came out in hundreds every night of the crusade in spite of the rain. Our prayer and watchfulness paid off.

As Christians, the Lord has made us watchmen (and women). He expects us to warn the people about the impending danger of living in sin. The Bible says:

> "I searched for a man among them who would build up the wall and stand in the gap before Me for the land, so that I would not destroy it; but I found no one. Thus I have poured out My indignation on them; I have consumed them with the fire of My wrath; their way I have brought upon their heads," declares the Lord GOD.
> —EZEKIEL 22:30–31

We are not expected to worry about whether the people will heed the warning or not as they will be held accountable for their decision. Our job is to blow the trumpet. However, if we refuse to warn the people when we are aware of the conditions of their hearts and the impending danger, God says He will require the blood of such from us. God's desire is to save all, but He will not compromise His justice and that's why He wants us to blow the trumpet anytime He speaks to us.

Moses was used mightily by God as a watchman. And the question is: are you willing to be used of God too? You might have failed in this regard in the past, but God is presenting you with another opportunity through this book to speak for Him to sinners around you. He is a gracious God and will empower you, for His mercy endures forever.

Prayer

My heavenly Father, I thank You for Your lovingkindness and mercy and for counting me worthy to be used as a watchman. In any way that I might have let You down in the past, I ask that You forgive me in Jesus' name. I ask that You give me the boldness to declare Your Word at all times in Jesus' name. I ask that You help me to listen attentively to You and see precisely what You are doing around me. Lord, anoint my mouth to speak Your Word with power and authority. I also ask that You prepare the hearts of the people You want to use me to reach. In Jesus' mighty name I pray, amen.

eight

MOSES—MAN OF INTEGRITY AND FAITH

OSES WAS USED mightily of God because he interceded constantly for the people he led. He acted
very well as a watchman, warning the people of
the impending danger. We have also established that he was
very humble, to the extent that it was written that he was more
humble than anyone else on the face of the earth at the time.
All these are the attributes that a person desiring to be used of
God must have. In addition to Moses' attributes, the Lord had
one more thing to say about him. The Bible says:

> He said, "Hear now My words: If there is a prophet
> among you, I, the LORD, shall make Myself known
> to him in a vision I shall speak with him in a dream.
> Not so, with My servant Moses, *He is faithful in all My
> household*; With him I speak mouth to mouth, Even
> openly, and not in dark sayings, And he beholds the
> form of the LORD. Why then were you not afraid To
> speak against My servant, against Moses?"
> —NUMBERS 12:6–8, EMPHASIS ADDED

According to the dictionary, *integrity* is the "quality or condition of being whole or undivided; completeness." It is sticking
to your "guns" in the face of distraction. Integrity is being

consistent in every situation. In other words, it is adhering to God's standards against all odds.

I know a Christian lady who worked for a big corporation. She had worked for the company for almost two decades, and everybody knew her as a very hard worker. According to her, she had been refused promotion a number of times just because she wouldn't go out with some top executives of the company. Some of her women colleagues with less qualification were occupying higher positions than her because they were willing to do anything to get recognition and positions. She mentioned that she had been advised to do the same thing, but she bluntly refused.

She recognized her body as the temple of the living God, and according to her, she was thankful and content with where the Lord had placed her and would not let her guard down no matter what. She believed that in God's time He makes all things beautiful. That is the type of attitude that is expected of a child of the kingdom. We should not serve God for what we can get from Him but because He is God. When you are a person of integrity, it is going to be difficult for God to pass you by without entrusting you with responsibilities. This Christian lady was later promoted and transferred to a different department where she found fulfillment.

Moses had the privilege of speaking with God face to face because he had integrity before God to the point that God entrusted him with all His house. That gave him unhindered access to God. How easy will our lives be when we can talk with God face to face? That means instant answer to our prayers. It means knowing the mind of God concerning any situation in our lives and having nothing hidden from us. When we have the opportunity to speak with God face to face, there will be no ambiguity; neither will there be any room for doubt because we have unhindered access to God. We cannot have unhindered access to God without integrity.

Moses did not only have integrity with God, he also had faith, and he was one of the men of old who received divine approval. (See Hebrews 11:2, 24–28.) Faith is believing God for what is naturally and humanly impossible. It is seeing and affirming what is yet to happen as having happened. According to the Bible, "faith is the assurance of things hoped for, the conviction of things not seen" (Heb. 11:1).

Each time I remember how the Lord sponsored my wedding, I marvel at how sincere faith in the Lord can produce tremendous miracles in the lives of his children. In Nigeria, March 1999, my fiancée and I were living away from each other as she worked in the eastern part of the country while I worked in Lagos (western part). Since her family lived in Lagos she came to celebrate Easter with them. Prior to coming for Easter, she had told me God spoke to her regarding our wedding and I had pressured her to tell me what God ministered to her, but she wouldn't. She promised to tell me when she came for Easter.

Immediately after we got to her house after she arrived in Lagos, my first question was, "What did the Lord speak to you?" She then told me the Lord said we would be getting married in May 1999. She told me she had struggled with the thought of getting married in two months and had been thinking maybe the Lord meant May 2000. I was speechless for a while, too, because at the time we had nothing to suggest we could be married in two months. We prayed and agreed that with God all things are possible.

A month later my fiancée and I received the news that we had won the diversity visa lottery and therefore had to get married in the following month (May 1999) so that we could complete and return the immigration forms back to the United

States. My wife (then fiancée) and I tried to give excuses why we could not get married in a month. By the time we joined God in what He was doing, we were already halfway through the month of May 1999, leaving us with less than two weeks to plan our wedding.

Since it was not about us, but about God and His faithfulness, He raised people who blessed us with money and materials needed for our marriage. We had about four hundred people at the wedding and more than four hundred at the reception. My pastor at the time said to me that the wedding could not have been better, even if we had a year to plan for it. When we agree with God's words, we are bound to see Him move the immovable out of our way.

It might have taken Moses a while to believe God for His words, but the moment he said yes to the Lord, he put all his faith in Him. Moses demonstrated faith on several occasions—from standing before Pharaoh and his officials in Egypt to stretching out his staff over the red sea. It would take a man of faith to believe God for those kinds of miracles.

Moses was a man of integrity and faith. He was really the Lord's chosen. But in spite of all these attributes, Moses still did not get to the Promised Land. What could have gone wrong? How did this mighty man of God miss the mark? I pray that the Lord will reveal Himself to you as we examine what went wrong in Moses' life.

PRAYER

Heavenly Father, I thank You for Your mercies upon me all the time. I am thankful to You for not giving up on me in those times when I have wavered. I ask You Lord at this moment to give me the courage from now on to stand for You no matter what the situation is, in Jesus' name. Father, I ask that You give me the patience to wait on You even when I don't understand what You are doing. I refuse to be a lukewarm Christian in Jesus' name. Heavenly Father, increase my faith and let every iota of doubt in me disappear in Jesus' name. I refuse to believe the report of the enemy, but the report of the Lord from now on. In Jesus' mighty name I pray, amen.

nine

SIGNIFICANCE OF PISGAH

REAPING THE CONSEQUENCES of our past actions is not always desirable, especially if those actions were not noble ones. We would like to sow one thing and reap another, but the Bible says in Galatians 6:7–8:

> Do not be deceived; God is not mocked, for whatever a man sows, this he will also reap. For the one who sows to his own flesh will from the flesh reap corruption, but the one who sows to the Spirit will from the Spirit reap eternal life.

That is the law of sowing and reaping. Oftentimes we don't care about some shortcomings in our lives just because they are not considered the "big" sins. The truth of the matter is that those things we consider little or irrelevant can hinder us from achieving God's purpose for our lives. Here is what the Bible says about it in Hebrews 12:1 (KJV):

> Wherefore seeing we also are compassed about with so great a cloud of witnesses, let us lay aside every weight, and the sin which doth so easily beset us, and let us run with patience the race that is set before us.

Looking at the above scripture again, it says we should lay aside every weight. What is the significance of weight in this context? It could be described as a hindering force. So the Bible is saying we should throw off everything that hinders. It may not look sinful, but as long as it can hinder you, as long as it can slow you down, you are being told to throw it off. It's interesting the Bible didn't say to throw off just one thing, but *everything* that hinders. There is no way we are going to run the race of life successfully as Christians if we carry weights on our backs. A runner always avoids weights because they can influence the outcome of the race in a negative way, in the sense that he/she may not achieve maximum potential. Is there any weight you are carrying now? I want to encourage you by God's Spirit to lay aside such weights, as there is no other way to achieve success in the Christian race but to give it your all. The good Lord can help you achieve that, but you must be willing.

Moses was called of God to lead the Israelites out of captivity in Egypt. He was empowered to do the job by God regardless of all his excuses. Moses, however, had some weights on him, sins which cling so closely. He failed to deal with these weights, and they resurfaced later in his ministry. Notwithstanding Moses' outstanding leadership and his unselfishness, the weights on him would not allow him to cross over to the other side from the top of Pisgah. Deuteronomy 3:23–28 (NIV, emphasis added) says:

> At that time I pleaded with the LORD: "O Sovereign LORD, you have begun to show to your servant your greatness and your strong hand. For what god is there in heaven or on earth who can do the deeds and mighty works you do? Let me go over and see the good land beyond the Jordan—that fine hill country and Lebanon." But because of you the LORD was angry with me and would not listen to me. "That is enough," the LORD said. "Do not speak to me anymore about this matter. *Go up to the top of Pisgah* and look west and

north and south and east. Look at the land with your own eyes, since you are not going to cross this Jordan. But commission Joshua, and encourage and strengthen him, for he will lead this people across and will cause them to inherit the land that you will see."

Did you notice that Moses did not confess his sins and neither did he ask God for forgiveness? Instead he blamed the Israelites for his plight. So, even though he praised God, forgiveness can only be obtained by genuine repentance. Was this the same Moses who moved the hand of God to action, who caused God to change His mind through his intercessions? Yes! This was the same Moses, but at this point, things had changed. The Lord was angry with him and had made up His mind. It was obvious Moses had been taken advantage of by the enemy and unfortunately, he did not realize it.

The devil always tries to take advantage of situations, especially if they have to do with a child of God. He tries as much as possible to perpetuate the same situation from one generation to another. There are people dealing with divorce in their generational line; the great-grandparents were divorced, the grandparents were divorced, and the current generation is also getting divorced. To some, it is a particular ailment (e.g., cancer, diabetes, arthritis, etc.) that has been in the family for generations. To some other people it may be poverty— nobody has ever been financially independent in the family. And the list is unending. The point is that the devil likes to keep us in bondage perpetually. Let's see an example of this in Bible. Genesis 12:10–13 says:

Now there was a famine in the land; so Abram went down to Egypt to sojourn there, for the famine was severe in the land. It came about when he came near to

> Egypt, that he said to Sarai his wife, "See now, I know that you are a beautiful woman; and when the Egyptians see you, they will say, 'This is his wife'; and they will kill me, but they will let you live. Please say that you are my sister so that it may go well with me because of you, and that I may live on account of you."

We need to be careful of the thoughts that we entertain in our hearts The Bible says in Proverbs 23:7, "As he thinketh in his heart, so is he" (KJV). Thoughts are very powerful. Your thoughts can determine who you become in life. That's why the devil is always seeking to control our thoughts; but the good news is that every Christian has available to him spiritual weapons that are mighty through God to take every thought captive to obey Christ. (See 2 Corinthians 10:4–5.) We should not be surprised then by what happened to Abram. He made up a lie prior to entering Egypt. What do you anticipate? What are your fears? If you do not bring those negative thoughts captive to obey Christ, I'm sorry they might come to pass. Genesis 12:14–19 says:

> It came about when Abram came into Egypt, the Egyptians saw that the woman was very beautiful. Pharaoh's officials saw her and praised her to Pharaoh; and the woman was taken into Pharaoh's house. Therefore he treated Abram well for her sake; and gave him sheep and oxen and donkeys and male and female servants and female donkeys and camels. But the LORD struck Pharaoh and his house with great plagues because of Sarai, Abram's wife. Then Pharaoh called Abram and said, "What is this you have done to me? Why did you not tell me that she was your wife? Why did you say, 'She is my sister,' so that I took her for my wife? Now then, here is your wife, take her and go."

Abram told a lie and this opened up a gateway to the spirit of lies, and a curse was released. Please note that sin will always open up a gateway to demonic attacks and curses. To prove that Abram had opened up a gateway to the spirit of lies, let's see what happened much later after the initial experience with Pharaoh. The Bible says in Genesis 20:1–2:

> Now Abraham journeyed from there toward the land of the Negev, and settled between Kadesh and Shur; then he sojourned in Gerar. Abraham said of Sarah his wife, "She is my sister" So Abimelech king of Gerar sent and took Sarah.

Have you noticed a pattern in Abraham's life? This was not normal. He was now under the influence of a lying spirit. The Bible speaks of the devil as the father of lies in John 8:44:

> You are of your father the devil, and you want to do the desires of your father. He was a murderer from the beginning, and does not stand in the truth, because there is no truth in him. Whenever he speaks a lie, he speaks from his own nature; for he is a liar, and the father of lies.

The devil is a smooth liar who sometimes comes in the form of an angel of light and many have become his victims. Lying is a sin because it is contrary to the nature of God; and if we find ourselves lying, then we need to quickly confess it to the Lord. When we fail to confess a sin, we may find ourselves doing it again and getting more comfortable with it. That does not mean the Lord is pleased with it. What we are doing is identifying with the devil. That means we are playing with fire and then stand the risk of being consumed by it.

Would you be surprised if I told you that Abraham passed this lying spirit to his son Isaac? Genesis 26:1 says, "Now there was a famine in the land, besides the previous famine that had occurred in the days of Abraham. So Isaac went to Gerar, to Abimelech king of the Philistines." Was this a coincidence or what? The same thing that happened to Abram in Genesis 12:10 was being played out again here. It looks to me as though the devil knows our weaknesses. It was a famine that led Abram in Genesis 12:10 to go to Egypt, and now there was a famine again in Isaac's time. Could you guess where Isaac was planning to go originally? The Bible has the answer in Genesis 26:2: "The LORD appeared to him and said, 'Do not go down to Egypt; stay in the land of which I shall tell you.'" So Isaac was planning on going down to Egypt. What is the spiritual significance of Egypt here? Egypt represents the land of slavery or bondage, the land of hardship, the land of forced labor, and the land of groaning in pain. To sum it up, it represents worldliness. But the Bible says in 1 John 2:16, "For all that is in the world, the lust of the flesh, and the lust of the eyes, and the pride of life, is not of the Father, but is of the world" (KJV).

Many of us were full of all that is in the world prior to getting saved. We were in bondage to sins. It is not surprising that many have gone down to Egypt (the world) as a result of "famine" in their lives. Famine here may be a lack, perceived delay to prayer, disappointment, loss of loved ones, and so on. For as long as we live in this world, there may be a famine, but going down to Egypt is not an option because when you go *down*, you lose your position in the heavenly places and you forfeit your privileges as a child of the kingdom. My challenge to you is, *do not go down to Egypt.*

Isaac was planning to go down to Egypt just like his father Abram, but the Lord stopped him and asked him to stay in

Gerar. However, the same lying spirit that took advantage of his father was hiding somewhere in him waiting to oppress him. Genesis 26:6–7 says, "So Isaac lived in Gerar. When the men of the place asked about his wife, he said, 'She is my sister,' for he was afraid to say, 'my wife,' thinking, 'the men of the place might kill me on account of Rebekah, for she is beautiful.'" Unbelievable! Isaac told the same lie that Abraham his father told. One big gateway to the attack of the enemy in our lives is fear. The devil often magnifies things because he wants us to feel intimidated, helpless, and eventually fearful so that he can have access to us since God has not given us the spirit of fear. (See 2 Timothy 1:7, KJV.) Have you noticed that when you are fearful, all kind of come to your mind? That is a red flag that the enemy is trying to attack you and that it's time to display the Lord's boldness and rebuke the devil in Jesus' name. Isaac could have asked God for help, but he didn't. The lying spirit was now perpetuating this curse through the generational line. Did you know that it took a determined struggle by Jacob (Isaac's son) with God for a change of name before this curse could be broken?

Just as with Moses, God's plan is to use His children to deliver the lost world, to save the dying souls and preach liberty to the oppressed, but the devil is not happy about it. His desire is to frustrate God's plan for our lives, and he will do everything to perpetuate what happened to Moses in the life of every child of God. He desires that the spirit of Pisgah operate in the life of God's children because he knows that we cannot fulfill divine destiny that way. Many mighty men of God have fallen victim to the spirit of Pisgah. There was a case of a man of God who did so many exploits in the kingdom only to fall into adultery after many years in the ministry. Stories like this are common.

The devil is moving around like a roaring lion seeking someone to devour, says 1 Peter 5:8.

Pisgah is used as a metaphor in this book and represents the following:

1. A place where destiny is cut short or destroyed

We have the power to influence our destiny and God will not be blamed for the outcome. The Bible says in Romans 8:29–30:

> For those whom He foreknew, He also predestined to become conformed to the image of His Son, so that He would be the firstborn among many brethren; and these whom He predestined, He also called; and these whom He called, He also justified; and these whom He justified, He also glorified.

The destiny of a man is "the will and purpose of God for that man."[1] It was God's plan for Moses to lead the Israelites to the Promised Land, but he threw away the opportunity by altering God's plan for his life. Moses' divine destiny was cut short at Pisgah.

2. A place where passionate plea is no longer appreciated

Desperation would only work to a certain degree. It may not always change your current situation for the better. Moses' plea was too late. The Lord specifically told him not to bring the issue up again.

3. A place of failure at the edge of success

There is a thin line between success and failure. Moses was so close to his breakthrough. He could actually see the Promised Land from the top of Pisgah, but was not able to get into it. Can you remember times in your life when you were so close

---

1   Quote by Reverend Dr. James G. Salako.

to getting something and yet missed it? If failure has been a pattern in your life, the spirit of Pisgah might be in operation and you need to do something about it.

4. A place of losing the fruit of one's labor

Moses toiled. He labored very hard, interceded fiercely, warned the people appropriately, yet he did not eat the fruit of his labor. When the spirit of Pisgah is operational in any life, one will always labor in vain.

5. A place of substitution

Moses was replaced with Joshua. When the spirit of Pisgah is operational in your life, you might constantly find yourself losing your position to someone else. You may find yourself qualified for something, yet someone else gets it.

6. A place of unrealized dream

Moses' dream of leading the Israelites to the Promised Land was not realized. He could only go as far as the top of Pisgah. When you constantly have your dream shattered, it might involve the spirit of Pisgah.

PRAYER

Heavenly Father, I receive power to control situations around me in Jesus' name. I frustrate and destroy every plan of the enemy to perpetuate any evil pattern in my life and family in Jesus' name. By the grace of God, I shall not go down to Egypt in Jesus' name. Because I serve a covenant-keeping God who has promised to be with me unto the end of the age, my dreams shall not be shattered in Jesus' name. I shall fulfill my purpose in life in Jesus' name. Amen.

ten

PATHWAYS TO PISGAH

W EIGHTS OR SINS that easily entangled the life of Moses were what prevented him from entering the Promised Land, and I believe by the time you are done reading this, you will be able to relate to Moses. There may be more, but we are just going to consider some of the easily recognizable ones.

ANGER

Anger in itself is not a sin, but it can lead to sin and the Bible warns us against it. The Bible says of Moses in Exodus 2:11– 12 (NIV):

> One day, after Moses had grown up, he went out to where his own people were and watched them at their hard labor. He saw an Egyptian beating a Hebrew, one of his own people. Glancing this way and that and seeing no one, he killed the Egyptian and hid him in the sand.

If we are not watchful and prayerful, the enemy could mess up our testimony in a single day. Moses might have been nursing resentment against the Egyptians for a while, but one day the resentment gave birth to anger and anger to murder. Here Moses was just trying to defend a fellow Hebrew, but it got out of hand and he killed the Egyptian. In an attempt to escape justice, Moses went from living in luxury in Pharaoh's palace to living as a nomad in Midian. He wandered in Midian for forty years, and the good Lord turned Midian into his training camp. He forgave him and was still able to use the situation for His glory. God can do the same thing in our life. Your current situation may be a grand design by God to get you to where you should be. He can forgive and turn your situation around if you ask Him.

The old saying that "A stitch in time saves nine" is very true. If we fail to deal with a problem now, we may find ourselves dealing with the consequences of the problem later. When anger becomes a pattern in any life, there is the need to cry unto God. Moses certainly had a problem with anger. He said in Exodus 11:8 (emphasis added):

> "All these your servants will come down to me and bow themselves before me, saying, 'Go out, you and all the people who follow you,' and after that I will go out." *And he went out from Pharaoh in hot anger.*

Do you know if it was possible for Moses to lay his hands on Pharaoh, he would probably have killed him also at that point? Anyone who's always having hot anger is a very dangerous person to stay around. The Bible is very clear. Proverbs 22:24–25 says, "Do not associate with a man given to anger; or go with a hot-tempered man, Or you will learn his ways, And find a snare for yourself." When you are a friend with a man given to anger, there is every tendency that you will learn his ways if you are not careful. It is usually said: "Show me your friends, and I will tell you who you are." Moses might have forgotten that he was just an instrument in God's hand and not God. All that God expected of him was to deliver His (God's) messages to Pharaoh through Aaron. Whether Pharaoh complied or not should have been God's business.

On another occasion, Moses went up to Mount Sinai to talk to God and the Lord gave him the Ten Commandments. The Bible says in Exodus 31:18, "When He had finished speaking with him upon Mount Sinai, He gave Moses the two tablets of the testimony, tablets of stone, written by the finger of God." Now Moses had been gone for a while, and the Israelites became impatient. They pressured Aaron to make them gods because, according to them, they did not know what the fate of Moses was. They probably thought he was dead and would not come down from the mountain. Exodus 32:2–4 says:

> Aaron said to them, "Tear off the gold rings which are in the ears of your wives, your sons, and your daughters, and bring them to me." Then all the people tore off the gold rings which were in their ears and brought them to Aaron. He took this from their hand, and fashioned it with a graving tool and made it into a molten calf; and they said, "This is your god, O Israel, who brought you up from the land of Egypt."

Though the Israelites were unaware of it, the Lord saw what they were doing and told Moses to go down to them. Exodus 32:7–8 says:

> Then the LORD spoke to Moses, "Go down at once, for your people, whom you brought up from the land of Egypt, have corrupted themselves. They have quickly turned aside from the way which I commanded them. They have made for themselves a molten calf, and have worshiped it and have sacrificed to it and said, 'This is your god, O Israel, who brought you up from the land of Egypt!'"

Do you know there is nothing you do that the Lord does not know about, even if you do it in secret? What are you hiding from God? What are those sins that no one else knows about? Well, God knows. In verse 15 of Exodus 32, Moses went down to the people. "Then Moses turned and went down from the mountain with the two tablets of the testimony in his hand, tablets which were written on both sides; they were written on one side and the other."

Why are the tablets of testimony being emphasized again? The answer is that they were very important treasures. They were written by the finger of God and given by God Almighty Himself to Moses. Things took a twist as Moses approached the people. Exodus 32:19 says, "And it came to pass, as soon as he came nigh unto the camp, that he saw the calf, and the dancing: and *Moses' anger waxed hot*, and he cast the tables out of his hands, and brake them beneath the mount" (KJV, emphasis added). Did you know that it took Moses forty days and forty nights of waiting before God without food or water before he got the tablets of the covenant? One would have thought Moses would do everything possible to protect the tablets of the covenant, but he didn't. When a man is under the influence of the spirit of anger, he can do anything without thinking about it. Moses' anger burned hot again, and he did a terrible thing. He broke the tablets, which were the work of God, into pieces. If this was an attempt by Moses to impress God, it certainly didn't work. This was not the first time the Israelites had sinned against God, and this latest sin was not bigger or smaller than the other sins they had committed. To God a sin is a sin. One thing stood out from Moses' act: breaking the tablets as a way of showing his disapproval of the people's behavior was not the right thing to do, in fact, it was a dishonor to God. As God's children, we will always have mountaintop experiences when we wait on Him in prayer and fasting and when our desires are always for Him. He will come closer and speak to us just as He did to Moses, but the key is, we need to watch what we do and say when we go down to the people from the mountaintop position. By the people, I mean the so-called sinners, the adulterers, the liars, the fornicators, and so on. We must ensure that we honor and glorify God, not dishonor Him.

Moses obviously did not deal with this anger problem. I want to emphasize again that when we don't deal with a sin at the initial stage, it will always lead to a greater sin. Moses' anger led him to murder and then to dishonor God before the people by breaking the tablets of testimony given to him by God. Anger is not the only weight discovered in the life of Moses, he was also a good complainer and that leads us to the next weight.

COMPLAINING

Moses tried as much as he could to avoid the call of God. He complained and gave reasons why he was not worthy of the task, but he eventually gave in to God. It was obvious when God met Moses at Midian, that he had a complaining problem. What is astonishing is that the problem resurfaced later in his ministry. I often wonder if we Christians know that our flesh and spirit are at war against each other. If we fail to deal with our flesh by living in the spirit, that same flesh will become a stumbling block to fulfilling God's purpose in our life, Galatians 5:16–18 says:

> But I say, walk by the Spirit, and you will not carry out the desire of the flesh. For the flesh sets its desire against the Spirit, and the Spirit against the flesh; for these are in opposition to one another, so that you may not do the things that you please. But if you are led by the Spirit, you are not under the Law.

The Bible makes it clear that even though we have given our life to God and have been called by Him, the desires of the sinful nature are still there. So, the antidote to these sinful desires is to live by the spirit. Would you do it? You have everything to gain, I promise! In Numbers 11:1–3 (NIV), the Bible says:

> Now the people complained about their hardships in the hearing of the LORD, and when he heard them his anger was aroused. Then fire from the LORD burned among them and consumed some of the outskirts of the camp. When the people cried out to Moses, he prayed to the LORD and the fire died down. So that place was called Taberah, because fire from the LORD had burned among them.

As a leader, when you notice a problem or weakness among the people you are leading, it will be a wise decision to spend time to teach the people on the issue. Moses used his fire fighting approach to solving a problem again. He asked God to stop His anger without asking Him to solve the problem by changing the hearts of the people. I believe God can do anything. If Moses had asked Him to change the hearts of the people, He would probably have done it. After all, the Bible says even the hearts of the kings are in His hands. Of course, the Israelites had not learned their lesson after the above episode. Numbers 11:4–6 (emphasis added) says:

> *The rabble* who were among them had greedy desires; and also the sons of Israel wept again and said, "Who will give us meat to eat? We remember the fish which we used to eat free in Egypt, the cucumbers and the melons and the leeks and the onions and the garlic, but now our appetite is gone. There is nothing at all to look at except this manna."

According to the dictionary, the *rabble* is a group of persons regarded with contempt. So the rabble according to the Bible passage above refers to a mixed crowd of Egyptians and others who had followed Israel out of Egypt. I think the church needs to watch out for the "rabble" in our midst. The rabble is always the first to criticize the pastor and church leadership, and they always lead a rebellion against God and His anointed. Unfortunately many true believers in many churches have joined such "rabble," causing damage to God's kingdom here on earth. In the passage above, the people followed in the steps of the rabble in their midst and started to complain again, thus provoking God to anger once more. At this point Moses just broke down, and his old complaining problem resurfaced. I hear you say that Moses was just being human. Well that's true. We all complain at one point or the other in our walk with God. We complain, challenge, and even ask God questions just as Moses did. However, one lesson stands out as we examine the following verses: it is the fact that the grace of God is sufficient for us in any situation. If He calls you to do something, rest assured that He has prepared you for the task and complaining can only rob you of His grace. Let's examine Moses' reaction to this latest revolt by the Israelites. Numbers 11:10–13 (emphasis added) says:

> Now Moses heard the people weeping throughout their families, each man at the doorway of his tent; and the anger of the LORD was kindled greatly, and Moses was displeased. So Moses said to the LORD, *"Why have You been so hard on Your servant? And why have I not found favor in Your sight, that You have laid the burden of all this people on me? Was it I who conceived all this people? Was it I who brought them forth, that You should say to me, 'Carry them in your bosom as a nurse*

carries a nursing infant, to the land which You swore to their fathers'? Where am I to get meat to give to all this people? For they weep before me, saying, 'Give us meat that we may eat!'"

Does the above sound familiar? Sometimes we get fed up with our situation and let our frustration take control. We begin to say things out of control and sometimes get into more trouble for it. Moses began to complain to God just like the people, asked questions, and in addition he accused God of setting him up.

If you think Moses was done letting out his frustrations, wait until you read the next verse. Numbers 11:14–15 (NIV, emphasis added) says:

I cannot carry all these people by myself; the burden is too heavy for me. If this is how you are going to treat me, *put me to death right now*—if I have found favor in your eyes—and do not let me face my own ruin.

Moses refused to intercede for the people; he pushed his own agenda instead. He wanted God to take care of him and made it known that it was urgent. He thought the burden was just too great to bear. He forgot the grace of God and was ready to abandon his ministry. He had all along proved to God that he was able to lead this people, and the Lord had reciprocated this by increasing his anointing for that purpose. What Moses did not know was that God gave him the anointing of more than seventy people. How did I know? Let's see what the Bible has to say. Numbers 11:16–17 (emphasis added):

The LORD therefore said to Moses, "Gather for Me seventy men from the elders of Israel, whom you know to be the elders of the people and their officers and bring them to the tent of meeting, and let them take their stand there with you. Then I will come down and speak with you there, *and I will take of the Spirit who is upon you, and will put Him upon them; and they shall bear the burden of the people with you, so that you will not bear it all alone."*

Moses got his wish but at the cost of his anointing. Please note that imparting others with your anointing does not reduce the anointing on you, just as imparting people with knowledge does not reduce one's knowledge. It just means they have what you have. Here God could have used Moses to impart the seventy men with his anointing and they would have had the same anointing that was upon Moses, but because Moses made it clear to God that he was ready to give up his call and God would not change His mind about His call on Moses, God gave Moses what he wanted just as He gave him Aaron to accompany him to Pharaoh. God came down by Himself and took *some* of the anointing upon Moses and put it upon the seventy so that they could bear the burden of the people with him. When you take *some* out of something, that thing will no longer be whole. He was no longer the old Moses; he lost some of his anointing and authority and thus his feet were properly positioned on the road to Pisgah.

PRAYER

Heavenly Father, I ask that You search my heart and see if there is any wickedness in me. I receive help from above to deal with every wrong attitude I have. Help me to be patient with everyone that I come in contact with. Let me not forget Your benefits, Father, and help me to rejoice in every situation. I pray this in Jesus' mighty name, amen.

eleven

UNDERESTIMATING THE ANOINTING

T HE THIRD PATHWAY to Pisgah discovered in the life of Moses was his underestimation of the anointing. The Holy Spirit is the third personality in the Trinity and His influence or presence upon one is often referred to as the anointing. The Lord Jesus Christ promised to send the Holy Spirit to His disciples before He was taken to heaven. Luke 24:49 says, "And behold, I am sending forth the promise of My Father upon you; but you are to stay in the city until you are clothed with power from on high." The Holy Spirit plays very important roles in the life of a believer, and it is right to say that there is nothing we can achieve without Him. Some of His workings include:

He empowers

The apostle Peter was a man easily given to intimidation as was evident when he denied Christ three times. (See Luke 22:34.) However, on the day of Pentecost when the Holy Spirit came upon the disciples, Peter spoke with such power and authority that about three thousand people gave their lives to Christ. (See Acts 2:14–40.) What made the difference in Peter's life was the Holy Spirit. Acts 1:8 says, "But you will receive power when the Holy Spirit has come upon you; and you shall be My witnesses both in Jerusalem, and in all Judea and Samaria, and even to the remotest part of the earth."

I am a testimony to what God can do with a willing vessel. I had accepted the opportunity to preach at the Reno-Sparks Gospel Mission (RSGM) as a volunteer. The RSGM ministers to the physical and spiritual needs of the homeless, the recovering drug addicts, and the needy. Only the Holy Spirit could have given me the kind of boldness and power that I had ministering to those precious people. My very first day at the Mission, fifteen people gave their lives to the Lord; and within a period of three months, more than one hundred and fifty souls had been saved. The testimonies were outstanding. Those who were bound were loosed, and many who were once addicted to drugs were set free and made Jesus the Lord of their lives. Our lives can never remain the same once the Holy Spirit comes upon us. We will speak with authority, and demons will tremble at the sound of our voice, in Jesus' name. In order to witness effectively as believers, we need the Holy Spirit.

He counsels

The importance of getting good counsel cannot be overemphasized. Having someone to guide us when we are confused and to encourage us when we are down is certainly a good idea, but the only one who can do it better than any man is the Holy Spirit. The Lord Jesus says in John 15:26, "When the Counselor comes, whom I will send to you from the Father, the Spirit of truth who goes out from the Father, he will testify about me" (NIV). The Holy Spirit is described as the Counselor and Comforter. What does this mean to believers? It means no matter what we may be going through, no matter what the condition is, even in the midst of adversity, the Holy Spirit will be there to lead us aright and comfort us. Every believer needs the Holy Spirit if we are to survive in this cruel world.

He reveals the truth

The Holy Spirit helps us to discern good from evil. He is the Spirit of truth that helps us to recognize falsehood. The Bible warns us not to believe every spirit but to test every spirit whether they are from God or not, because many false prophets are in the world. (See 1 John 4:1.) This is the task that only the Holy Spirit can accomplish in us. It is unfortunate that many believers have become complacent and no longer recognize falsehood. Some so-called believers will even argue that we are all serving the same god as other religions. Well, the Bible says in 1 John 4:2–3:

> By this you know the Spirit of God: every spirit that confesses that Jesus Christ has come in the flesh is from God; and every spirit that does not confess Jesus is not from God; this is the spirit of the antichrist, of which you have heard that it is coming, and now it is already in the world.

Without the Holy Spirit we will remain in the dark and the truth will be far from us.

He instructs

In the book of Acts 1:1–2, Luke wrote, "In my former book, Theophilus, I wrote about all that Jesus began to do and to teach until the day he was taken up to heaven, after giving instructions through the Holy Spirit to the apostles he had chosen" (NIV). Here the Lord Jesus gave instructions to the disciples through the Holy Spirit. Do you need instructions from God? The Holy Spirit is the key. We do not hear from Him because we have refused to let Him have His way. We consult God after making up our minds on what we are going to do, and, of course, we cannot hear His instructions under that circumstance. It is expedient that we give Jesus Christ the totality of

99

our life and let Him instruct us by the Holy Spirit. Our life cannot remain the same.

We have considered some of the works of the Holy Spirit, and by now I'm sure you realize how important it is to allow the Holy Spirit to have His way in our lives. Moses was filled with the Holy Spirit to overflowing, and the anointing upon him was that of at least seventy-one people until he pushed it too far with God. Numbers 11:25 (emphasis added) says:

> Then the LORD came down in the cloud and spoke to him; and *He took of the Spirit* who was upon him and placed Him upon the seventy elders. And when the Spirit rested upon them, they prophesied. But they did not do it again.

Some is defined by the dictionary as "a quantity of a whole." When you take "some" out of a thing, the remainder will no longer be whole. The implication of the passage we just read is that, after God took some quantity out of the spirit that was upon Moses and distributed it upon the seventy elders, the spirit upon Moses was no longer whole and Moses could no longer function fully in the capacity in which he had functioned all this while. Moses underestimated the Lord's anointing and lost some of it, and the end result was not good.

God is holy and cannot tolerate sin or dwell in a sinful vessel. Do you feel as if the Holy Spirit is no longer with you? Have you grieved the Holy Spirit so that He no longer speaks to you? My challenge to you is to ask for forgiveness right now. Do it in Jesus' name and you will experience Him once more. Failure to do so will only set you on the course to Pisgah.

LIVING IN GOD'S PERMISSIVE WILL

Living in God's permissive will can be dangerous and most of the time will lead to regret. In 1 Samuel chapter 8, the Israelites asked for a king because they wanted to be like all other nations around them. They got their wish and the Lord gave them Saul, even though He had no intention of doing so originally. At the end of the day, it turned out to be a big mistake on the part of the Israelites and they suffered the consequences of their actions.

It was obvious the Lord meant for Moses to go to Egypt alone, but after bothering God with his complaints, he was eventually given Aaron as his mouthpiece. Do you remember the role Aaron played while Moses was up on Mount Sinai with God? Exodus 32:2–6 says:

> Aaron said to them, "Tear off the gold rings which are in the ears of your wives, your sons, and your daughters, and bring them to me." Then all the people tore off the gold rings which were in their ears and brought them to Aaron. He took this from their hand, and fashioned it with a graving tool and made it into a molten calf; and they said, "This is your god, O Israel, who brought you up from the land of Egypt." Now when Aaron saw this, he built an altar before it; and Aaron made a proclamation and said, "Tomorrow shall be a feast to the LORD." So the next day they rose early and offered burnt offerings, and brought peace offerings; and the people sat down to eat and to drink, and rose up to play.

The same Aaron who was called to assist Moses was the one who made an idol for the Israelites here. As a result of Aaron's act, Moses acted in anger and broke the two tables of the testimony given to him by God. When we take anything less than God's perfect will, what we are saying is that we are ready to face the challenges that may result from such action ourselves. Since we don't want this to happen to us, it is then important for us to pray that the will of God be done at all times in our lives.

Breaking Faith With God

Watch out for what you do when under pressure, because your action may make or mar you. Moses found himself acting under pressure, and he wished it had never happened.

On another occasion in the wilderness, specifically in the desert of Zin, there was no water for the people to drink. As usual, the people quarreled with Moses and said all kinds of terrible things. Moses did what he had always done. He went to God and worshipped Him by falling face down, and the Lord appeared in His glory and gave him instruction. Numbers 20:6 says, "Then Moses and Aaron came in from the presence of the assembly to the doorway of the tent of meeting and fell on their faces. Then the glory of the LORD appeared to them." When we fall on our face to worship God, something unusual must happen. In the case of Moses and Aaron, the glory of the Lord came down. Sometimes the reason the glory of God does not appear to us believers is because we are too high: we stand when we are supposed to fall on our faces. By this I mean we are too proud, we don't want to get our outfits dirty and sometimes we don't want people around us to think we are going too far. Well, there is an opportunity lost when we do that—we may never experience what it means to be in the presence of the Lord Almighty. When we bring ourselves low by falling on our face, when we humble ourselves, His glory is bound to appear.

God was honored when Moses fell on his face. He accepted Moses' invitation for fellowship, and He spoke to him. Numbers 20:8–10 (emphasis added) says:

> "Take the rod; and you and your brother Aaron assemble the congregation and *speak to the rock* before their eyes, that it may yield its water. You shall thus bring forth water for them out of the rock and let the congregation and their beasts drink." So Moses took the rod from before the LORD, just as He had commanded him; and Moses and Aaron gathered the assembly before the rock. And he said to them, "Listen now, you rebels; shall we bring forth water for you out of this rock?"

Coming from Nigeria, West Africa, I have not seen a shepherd without a rod in his hand. The Fulanis (a Nigerian tribe) in the north of Nigeria are predominantly shepherds (rearing cattle), and they are usually referred to as nomads. These nomads move with their herd of cattle from one place to the other looking for green pastures. To a nomad, the rod is the steering wheel by which the herd is controlled. A single nomad with a rod in his hand can control a big herd. The rod is used to guide and lead the herd to green pastures. The rod is also used to control the herd so that the cattle don't go astray. Sometimes when a member of the herd is straying, you will see the nomad raise his rod and strike the straying member. The straying member will quickly fall in line and continue on the same course as others. On other occasions all that the nomad needs to do to get the attention of a straying member is to raise his rod, and that is enough to get him back on the correct course. The rod can also be used to ward off any threat to the herd. The nomad's authority over the herd lies in his rod and he can use it in different ways to achieve the same purpose. Moses' rod or staff symbolized his authority over the people, and the Lord had used the rod in different ways. It once turned into a snake that swallowed the magicians' snakes. It turned the water in the Nile to blood, and on another occasion it parted the Red Sea when it was stretched out to it. The rod had also been used as an instrument in bringing provision to the people. (See Exodus 17:6.) Once again the Lord commanded him to take the rod and he did, but what did he do with the rod? When you go to the Lord in times of need, He places his rod in your hand, which symbolizes His authority over that need, but the question is: What do you do with the Lord's rod in your hand? As for Moses, he did the unexpected, and it turned out to be a very costly mistake. Numbers 20:11 says, "Then Moses lifted up his hand and struck the rock twice with his rod; and water came forth abundantly, and the congregation and their beasts drank."

Do you remember the instruction God gave Moses and Aaron in Numbers 20:8? God said to speak unto the rock before their eyes and it will pour out its water. Moses probably took the Lord for granted. He had struck the rock at Horeb before and water had come out. (See Exodus 17:5–6.) He probably did not see any reason to do it in a different way at this time, but we serve a dynamic God who is unlimited in His ways. That is why we need to come before Him with our hearts renewed, so that we may pay attention to everything He says. Even though Moses hit the rock not once but twice with total disregard for the Lord's instruction, the Lord still brought out water. As a leader in the church, people may still see you as a miracle worker and you may still be doing things that are bringing provision unto the people, but my question to you is: are you doing it God's way?

In the case of Moses, the Lord still protected His integrity. Because of His love and faithfulness to His words, He brought forth water. However the Lord was not happy about his outright disobedience, therefore He decreed that neither Moses nor Aaron would enter the Promised Land. Numbers 20:12 says, "But the LORD said to Moses and Aaron, 'Because you have not believed Me, to treat Me as holy in the sight of the sons of Israel, therefore you shall not bring this assembly into the land which I have given them.'" The Lord also reiterated His reasons for disallowing Moses from entering the Promised Land shortly before Moses died. In Deuteronomy 32:51 He said, "Because you broke faith with Me in the midst of the sons of Israel at the waters of Meribah-kadesh, in the wilderness of Zin, because you did not treat Me as holy in the midst of the sons of Israel."

Breaking faith with God means to trespass against God. According to the dictionary, in law, *trespass* means "to commit an unlawful injury to the person, property or rights of another, with actual or implied force or violence." God recorded hitting the rock as a trespass because it was an act of physical violence against God. Why was the loving God so tough on Moses? The answer is simply because of the rock. It is because Moses' action involved the rock and you will see it yourself as we consider what the Bible has to say about the Rock. First Corinthians 10:3–4 says, "They all ate the same spiritual food and drank the same spiritual drink; for they drank from the *spiritual rock* that accompanied them, *and that rock was Christ*" (NIV, emphasis added). Romans 9:33 says, "As it is written, 'See, I lay in Zion a stone that causes men to stumble and *a rock that makes them fall*, and the one who trusts in him will never be put to shame'" (NIV, emphasis added). The Rock is our Lord Jesus Christ. Do you agree that Moses went too far? Why would Moses do that? It was obvious Moses was under a lot of pressure from the people, and the pressure was probably too much for him. Should Moses have been under that much pressure? Maybe not! Moses might have forgotten that his anointing had been reduced and distributed among seventy other Israelite elders to help him carry the burden. It is important that leaders in the body of Christ delegate assignments to those we have raised and impacted with God's anointing upon us. God's anointing upon us is not for us so that we can show off, but for the church so that we can all be effective as a body. God works in diverse ways, and He chooses to do things the way He likes them done. We will only produce the desired result and be blessed when we act in obedience and believe His word by faith.

Inability to Uphold Holiness

God gave one more reason why He was tough on Moses and did not allow him to enter the Promised Land. The Lord himself said in Deuteronomy 32:51 that Moses did not revere Him as holy in the midst of the people of Israel by his action. It is so easy for us to blame Moses for doing this, but before you do that, I have a question for us as Christians: are we upholding God's holiness among the people—the people we work with, our family members, friends and neighbors? God's expectation of us is to uphold His holiness among all these people. We see that their lifestyles do not glorify God, yet we do not care enough to declare and introduce them to God. Our excuse is that we don't want to hurt their feelings or impose our faith on them. We cannot uphold God's holiness if we are not holy; we cannot uphold his holiness if He is not first in our lives; we cannot uphold God's holiness if Jesus Christ is not Lord of our lives. My challenge to us is to let the Lord Jesus Christ have His way in our lives because the moment we let Him, He will begin to guide and order our steps all the time. Our focus will be on fulfilling His purpose for our lives, and heaven will be our goal. That way, we cannot miss it!

PRAYER

Heavenly Father, forgive me in every way I might have sinned against You and give me the grace to abide in You. Lord, I pray that no contrary spirit shall prosper in my life, because I belong to You. I shall not lose the anointing of God upon my life. I declare that I shall live in the perfect will of God for my life. I also proclaim that I shall be a true ambassador of Christ from now on. (See 2 Corinthians 5:20.) I pray all these things in Jesus' mighty name, amen.

twelve

DEFEATING THE SPIRIT
OF PISGAH

THE SPIRIT OF Pisgah may have crawled into our lives, family, or church. Therefore, defeating it must be our goal. We have discussed in the previous chapter the pathways to Pisgah. If we would avoid the road to Pisgah as seen in the life of Moses, there is the need for us to revere and honor God no matter what we may be going through, for He is there with us and will see us through.

I remember long ago, while I was still living in Nigeria, I used to do a lot of bus evangelism (witnessing on the bus is allowed in the southern part of Nigeria). One day, I was returning home from work after a very hectic day. I was so tired and worn out, especially with the chaotic lifestyle of struggling to get a bus at peak time in Lagos, Nigeria. I eventually got on a bus, and as I was settling down in my seat, the Lord prompted me to witness to the people on the bus. It was the last thing I wanted to hear or do. I started to rationalize and say to myself: "I won't be able to speak loud enough for the people to hear." I also thought if I did, it would aggravate my situation, as I had a headache. Lo and behold! While I was still contemplating whether or not to preach, another passenger on the bus got up and started to preach. I felt so bad, especially since I had preached so many times before when I had been prompted. The Lord spoke to me saying that He knew I was tired but just wanted to let me know that His strength is made perfect in my weakness. I learned a great lesson.

Problems in our lives may sometimes seem overwhelming. Taking our difficult situations to God and asking for guidance will be the right way to go. I can assure you that He will not leave you without His comforting words. He will also give directions as to what to do. I remember losing my job and having to struggle financially for the next several months. Five months down the line we were left with the only option of cashing my 401(k) so we could pay our bills for that month. The following month we had practically nothing left, but the Lord kept assuring us that everything would be all right. Well, we believed Him for His words because He is faithful. We know that His words shall not return to Him void. We had to borrow some money in order to pay our bills for that month. In the midst of that turbulence the Lord gave me a word to go to World Harvest Bible College in Columbus, Ohio. I shared with my wife, and I was shocked when she said that she had known that's where I would go. Since we did not know where Columbus was, we had to go on the Internet to look at the map. I had this thought in my mind that it was near Arizona but was surprised to see that it is in the Midwest. The Lord blessed us through the sale of our house and other possessions and that was the provision He made for us to start with in Columbus.

The need to refrain and control our anger in order to prevent mistakes that could have been avoided cannot be overemphasized if we are to defeat the spirit of Pisgah. It is not a sin to be angry, but it becomes a sin when we refuse to control it. The Holy Spirit is a gentle Spirit, and if He truly lives in us, then we must be subject to Him. How many churches have broken apart due to words spoken in anger by feuding members? If we are to achieve the plan of God for our lives, we must totally yield to the Holy Spirit, and He will cause us to bring forth the fruit of the Spirit; which is love, joy, peace, patience, kindness, goodness, faithfulness, gentleness, and self control. The Bible declares that against such there is no law. (See Galatians 5:22–23.)

Appreciating God's anointing upon us is also important in defeating the spirit of Pisgah. Losing God's anointing can only lead to Pisgah. We cannot fulfill God's purpose if we are not anointed for it. Yokes can only be destroyed by the anointing. Acts 10:38 says, "How God anointed Jesus of Nazareth with the Holy Spirit and power, and how he went around doing good and healing all who were under the power of the devil, because God was with him" (NIV). We will only be able to do good and heal all who are oppressed of the devil by the anointing. So protect God's anointing upon your life. Do not lose Him.

Equally emphasized is the need to avoid deliberately trespassing against God. It always leads to destruction. Sin is a poison and a destroyer. It can defeat and destroy the purpose of God for our lives. It brings about separation between us and God. We need to run away from sin! The Bible says in 1 Thessalonians 5:22, "Abstain from every form of evil." It is unfortunate that many Christians now take the grace of God for granted. We commit premeditated sin believing that God will be merciful afterward. Galatians 6:7 says, "Do not be deceived, God is not mocked; for whatever a man sows, this he will also reap." If we would hate sin with perfect hatred, God's holiness will rub on us and we will be able to see Him in everything we do. After all, the Bible says without holiness, no man shall see God. (See Hebrews 12:14.)

Other keys to avoiding the road to Pisgah include:

Avoiding people pressure

To succeed in our ministry or anything the Lord has committed into our hands, we need to always seek the mind of God. Moses' bad reputation was a great concern to him when God called him. As it was with Moses, our past reputation is often a source of concern when God calls us. The good news is that the Bible says in 2 Corinthians 5:17, "Therefore if any man be in Christ, he is a new creature: old things are passed away; behold, all things are become new" (KJV). People may call us names when we make God the first priority in our lives and may seek to discourage us. One thing we need to know is that the devil does not want us to succeed and will use all the means at his disposal to bring us down. We need to stay focused and refuse to yield to any ungodly influence. The Lord Jesus says in Matthew 5:10–12:

> Blessed are those who have been persecuted for the sake of righteousness, for theirs is the kingdom of heaven. Blessed are you when people insult you and persecute you, and falsely say all kinds of evil against you because of Me. Rejoice and be glad, for your reward in heaven is great; for in the same way they persecuted the prophets who were before you.

What an incredible word of encouragement from the Lord! Therefore, we should let our focus be on the great reward that is awaiting us in heaven. Moses yielded to the pressure from the people and the end result was not good. When you are under pressure, seek God's help, tap into His grace, and He will see you through.

Aggressive prayer

This is the main key to defeating the spirit of Pisgah. The Bible says in James 5:16, "Confess your faults one to another, and pray one for another, that ye may be healed. The effectual fervent prayer of a righteous man availeth much" (KJV). Don't be intimidated by your situation, you have the righteousness of our Lord Jesus Christ. Put the enemy on his toes by your constant and unrelenting prayers and release the power of God into your situation.

Nigeria is a soccer-loving nation. Soccer is referred to as football in most of the world outside of the United States. Soccer is played in two halves for a total of ninety minutes. During halftime following the first half, the teams take a rest, reevaluate their situation, and map out new plans in order to win the game. Whenever the Nigeria national football team— the "Super Eagles"—is playing a big match, you will be able to tell easily, especially in the big cities as traffic will be light while the match is taking place. Fans who may not be able to go to the stadium to watch the game live will stay glued to their television sets at home until the match is over.

It is a common saying among Nigerians that the best form of defense is attack. What this means is that when you put your opponents under constant pressure, you stand a good chance to disorganize them. In soccer it is believed that your opponent's defense is bound to crumble under intense pressure and you stand a great chance of scoring more goals against the opponent under such circumstance, which leads to victory.

The above scenario was perfectly demonstrated by the Nigerian Under-21 national team during the 1989 Federation of International Football Associations (FIFA) World Cup tournament held in Saudi Arabia. The Nigerian team played Russia in the quarterfinal and was trailing by four goals to none with half an hour remaining in the match. It was the second half, and nobody gave the Nigerian team any chance at that point. When all hope had been lost, the Nigerian team found their strength and started to put pressure on the Russians who had shifted into full-time defensive tactics believing they had the game as good as won. When the pressure became intense, the Russian defense gave in and the Nigerian team scored a goal. A second goal was scored by the Nigeria side a few minutes later. The Russian defense was rattled. They became disoriented and before they knew it, the Nigerian side had scored two more goals to bring the score level. It was a miracle! The Nigerian side scored four goals in twenty-four minutes and eventually won the game on tie-breaker penalty kicks.

God has given us power to trample over Satan and it is only by praying consistently that we can perpetually subdue him.

There is a song that says:

> Prayer is the key
> Prayer is the key
> Prayer is the master key
> Jesus started with prayer and ended with prayer
> Prayer is the master key

Why do we need to pray? Well the answer is simple. The Lord Jesus Christ commanded it. Matthew 26:41 says, "Keep watching and praying that you may not enter into temptation; the spirit is willing, but the flesh is weak." We need to pray because the devil is here on earth. The Lord Jesus Christ Himself prayed all the time while He was here on earth. He was tempted by the devil, yet He overcame him by the word of God.

A prayerless Christian is a powerless Christian. There is little you can do in the kingdom walk without prayers. First Peter 5:8–9 says:

> Be of sober spirit, be on the alert. Your adversary,
> the devil, prowls around like a roaring lion, seeking
> someone to devour. But resist him, firm in your faith,

knowing that the same experiences of suffering are being accomplished by your brethren who are in the world.

The devil is seeking to devour you. He is seeking to destroy your destiny and take advantage of you and your situation. The devil has demons working for him day and night, but I have good news for you! The Bible says in Luke 10:17, "The seventy returned with joy, saying, 'Lord, even the demons are subject to us in Your name.'" These were the seventy people appointed by the Lord Jesus Christ to go in twos to preach the gospel. Here they returned sharing their testimony of how the demons were submitting to them. What was the Lord's response to them? Luke 10:18–19 (KJV) says:

And He said unto them, I beheld Satan as lightning fall from heaven. Behold, I give unto you power to tread on serpents and scorpions, and over all the power of the enemy: and nothing shall by any means hurt you.

How should we pray? Below are some ways by which Jesus prayed and how He expects us to pray:

Pray aloud

I want to quickly point out that there is nothing wrong with praying silently for as long as one's mind is in it. But I firmly believe that when we speak out God's words in prayers, it builds faith in us and helps us to pray from our heart. Hebrews 5:7 says, "During the days of Jesus' life on earth, he offered up prayers and petitions with loud cries and tears to the one who could save him from death, and he was heard because of his reverent submission" (NIV).

Pray all night

Spiritual wickedness in the heavenly places operates mostly at night while people are sleeping. It is no coincidence that we serve a God who neither sleeps nor slumbers. He watches over us at all times, and since He has given us authority and dominion over the power of darkness, He expects us to pray in the nighttime also. My wife and I have experienced God's visitation more when we pray during the night. This is not to say that God doesn't answer prayers at any other time, but it takes determination, boldness, and desperation to get up and pray during the night when the activities of the enemy are on the increase—and God honors that. Luke 6:12 says, "It was at this time that He went off to the mountain to pray, and He spent the whole night in prayer to God." Jesus prayed all night and we are expected to do same if we are to walk in power and authority.

Pray early in the morning

What a better time to set the activities for the day than early in the morning. Our Lord Jesus Christ prayed early in the morning when He was here on earth. Mark 1:35 says, "Very early in the morning, while it was still dark, Jesus got up, left the house and went off to a solitary place, where he prayed" (NIV). Jesus set the course of the day by His early prayers. No wonder He moved in power and authority all day long as people thronged in to see him.

Pray at all times

Whether things are going right or not, my challenge to you is to pray. First Thessalonians 5:17 says, "Pray without ceasing." Our strength is derived from the Lord. As such, we will only be filled with God's power when we spend time with Him.

Conditions to satisfy when we pray include:

Pray in Jesus' name

All authority in heaven and on earth has been given to our Lord Jesus Christ. (See Matthew 28:18.) Only his name brings defeat to any contrary situation in our lives. Philippians 2:9–11 (NIV) says:

> Therefore God exalted him to the highest place and gave him the name that is above every name, that at the name of Jesus every knee should bow, in heaven and on earth and under the earth, and every tongue confess that Jesus Christ is Lord, to the glory of the Father.

Pray by faith

Without faith it is impossible to please God, declares Hebrews 11:6. Faith is very vital to having our prayer answered. We must believe the spoken word of God regarding our situations. God is ever faithful. He will do whatever He has spoken, and there is the need for us to "approach the throne of grace with confidence, so that we may receive mercy and find grace to help us in our time of need" (Heb. 4:16, NIV).

What else do you need to know? The Lord Himself has told you that you now have the power to deal with the devil and his demons, but this can only happen by prayer and fasting. There are all kinds of demons, but when you pray in the name of Jesus they must bow out of your situation. God has highly exalted the name of our Lord Jesus Christ and nothing is impossible when you pray in His name.

On one occasion during Jesus' time, a boy possessed by a demon was brought to the disciples of the Lord Jesus Christ, but they were unable to cast out the evil spirit. Mark 9:17–18 says:

> And one of the crowd answered Him, "Teacher, I brought You my son, possessed with a spirit which

makes him mute; and whenever it seizes him, it slams him to the ground and he foams at the mouth, and grinds his teeth and stiffens out. I told Your disciples to cast it out, and they could not do it."

Jesus rebuked and cast the spirit out of him. Mark 9:25–27 says:

> When Jesus saw that a crowd was rapidly gathering, He rebuked the unclean spirit, saying to it, "You deaf and mute spirit, I command you, come out of him and do not enter him again." After crying out and throwing him into terrible convulsions, it came out; and the boy became so much like a corpse that most of them said, "He is dead!" But Jesus took him by the hand and raised him; and he got up.

Note that the Lord Jesus addressed the spirit by its name (dumb and deaf spirit). He then commanded the spirit to go out and never enter into the boy again, and the spirit obeyed him. There are several spirits prevalent in our society, but rather than calling them by their names and rebuking them, we have chosen to give them excuses by the reason of medical science. I perceive that if the boy with the dumb and deaf spirit had lived in our time today, we would have given his condition a name, something like "deafdumbiolassaphitis." Ridiculous! Isn't it? We have seen violence in an unprecedented manner, suicide and immorality among teenagers at a rate we have never seen before, and the airwaves are being used to pervert the truth of the word of God. People want to hear half-truths, and yet we are not eager to talk about these. We have a responsibility to shine the light to the utter darkness of this world. Remember, the Bible says we are the light of the world. Matthew 5:14–16 says:

You are the light of the world. A city set on a hill cannot be hidden; nor does anyone light a lamp and put it under a basket, but on the lampstand, and it gives light to all who are in the house. Let your light shine before men in such a way that they may see your good works, and glorify your Father who is in heaven.

Jesus' disciples were surprised by the way the demon obeyed Him, so they engaged the Lord Jesus in a private conversation after the encounter. Mark 9:28 says, "And when he was come into the house, his disciples asked him privately, 'Why could not we cast him out?'" (KJV). Jesus answered them in verse 29, "And he said unto them, This kind can come forth by nothing, but by prayer and fasting" (KJV). You cannot cast out demons if you are afraid of them and refuse to use your authority. Jesus spoke out boldly any time He had an encounter with demons.

I used to be in the deliverance team of my local church back in Nigeria. I have been in situations where demons spoke through their subjects. I remember very well on one occasion praying for a sister who was being violently thrown around by a demon. The Holy Spirit instructed me to ask for the demon's name, and I did. The demon spoke through the sister and said his name was the spirit of death. I then began to rebuke the spirit of death and the sister was eventually delivered. I later asked her what happened while she was on the floor and she did not remember anything. Remember the Lord Jesus said in His words that we would do greater things than He did. His power is available to us today.

Many people get so caught up in religion and tradition that they think there is nothing like demons, and that praying against them is going too far. If you want to be mightily used of God, you must discard religion and tradition. Believe God's word and listen to His voice. That is the only way to do exploits for Him. Prayers, when accompanied with fasting, can do a lot of damage to the kingdom of darkness. According to the dictionary, *fasting* is the act or practice of abstaining from or eating very little food. Did I hear you say that you cannot fast? That is the lie of the devil. You can do it! The Bible says in Philippians 4:13, "I can do all things through Him who strengthens me." Start with skipping a meal, then two meals or the whole day. It is a good spiritual exercise that brings about unimaginable reward. The Lord's grace is sufficient for you. Fasting humbles you. It puts you in a position to receive from God. When you go without something for the sake of seeking His face, God cannot do without honoring the trust that you have in Him. James 4:10 tells us to humble ourselves before the Lord, and He will lift us up. Fasting requires a lot of discipline. Don't be surprised that the day that you choose to fast is the same day you wake up hungry. What do you need to do? Crucify your flesh. You may fast for a few hours, days, or several weeks. Let the Spirit of the Lord lead you on the length of the fast, and watch God move on your behalf. Pray in the name of Jesus, and stubborn situations will change in your favor.

PRAYER

Lord Jesus, strengthen me against every opposition to Your will in my life. I receive divine power and ability to pray in Jesus' name. Lord Jesus, give me the grace and ability to wait on You in fasting and prayer and let signs and wonders accompany my words as I declare them. I shall experience unbelievable miracles that only You can bring in my ministry. I pray in Jesus' mighty name, amen.

CONCLUSION

THE ROAD TO Pisgah is a treacherous road, and its destination is not desirable. It is the road to regret, it is the road to defeat, and it is also the road to failure at the edge of breakthrough. You have a choice not to be on this road, and if you are already on the road, you now have the power to pull yourself off it. You can put a stop to the activities of the spirit of Pisgah in your life in the name of Jesus. We are in a battle, and we need the whole armor of God in order to be perfectly protected and achieve victory. We need to do everything in our power in order to stand firm and maintain our victory. The Bible made it clear in Ephesians 6:11–13 (KJV):

> Put on the whole armour of God, that ye may be able to stand against the wiles of the devil. For we wrestle not against flesh and blood, but against principalities, against powers, against the rulers of the darkness of this world, against spiritual wickedness in high places. Wherefore take unto you the whole armour of God, that ye may be able to withstand in the evil day, and having done all, to stand.

Beloved, as you have read above, our fight is not against flesh and blood, but against principalities, powers, rulers of this dark world, and spiritual hosts of wickedness in the heavenly places. If you truly look at what is happening in our world today, I'm sure you will agree that this is the truth. There is no need to be fearful, because you have the whole armor of God available to you. However there is no armor for your back. (See Ephesians 6:14–18.) This means that we cannot look back in this battle. Each time you look back, you are exposing yourself to danger. Some have turned their back against God, got hit by the devil, and have not been fortunate enough to recover. I challenge you to stand from this day on in Jesus name.

Would you pray this prayer with me if you have never given your life to Jesus? Say:

> *Dear Lord, I thank You for Your death for me on the cross at Calvary, and I thank You for making it possible for me to come to Your knowledge. I confess all my sins this day, and I receive the grace to live a life that is pleasing unto You from this moment on. I ask You to be Lord of my life and to guide me by Your Holy Spirit in all I shall do from now on. Thank You for answering my prayer, in Jesus' name, amen.*

Now pray this prayer out loud with all your heart and I believe the Lord will touch your situation and put a stop to every activity of the enemy in your life in Jesus name:

> *Heavenly Father, I thank You this day for an opportunity to commune with You and demonstrate Your power. I thank You because of Your goodness, Your mercy, and Your compassion upon me. I thank You because You have absolute power and authority to do all things, and You have also made that same power available to me, Your child. I pray this day that every situation contrary to Your will in my life will begin to bow to Your power now in Jesus' name.*
>
> *Lord Jesus, It is written in the Book of Matthew 7:7 that we should ask and it will be given unto us,*

that we should seek and we will find and that we should knock and it shall be opened unto us. I ask this day, that everything I say shall come to pass in Jesus' name.

It is written in Matthew 16:19 that You have given me the keys to the kingdom of heaven, that whatever I bind on earth shall be bound in heaven, and whatever I loose on earth shall be loosed in heaven; therefore, I bind every demon assigned to trouble me now with chains that can never be broken, in Jesus' name.

It is also written in the Book of Mark 16:17–18, "These signs will accompany those who have believed: in My name they will cast out demons, they will speak with new tongues; they will pick up serpents, and if they drink any deadly poison, it will not hurt them; they will lay hands on the sick, and they will recover." Therefore, I exercise my authority in Christ and I bind every demon assigned by the devil to trouble me. I cast such demons out of my life and situation into the abyss now, never to come back into my life, in Jesus' name. I plead the blood of Jesus upon my life, and I ask that the mark of Jesus be vivid upon my spirit, soul, and body from now on. It is written in 1 Chronicles 16:21–22 and Psalm 105:14–15: "He permitted no man to oppress them, and He reproved kings for their sakes, saying, 'Do not touch My anointed ones, and do My prophets no harm.'" According to the Word of the Lord, I now declare my life a no-go area for the devil and his agents from now on in Jesus' name. Lord, I ask for Your Holy Spirit to come upon me now, and to dwell with me from now on. I now proclaim and declare freedom in every area of my life, for it is *written in 2 Corinthians 3:17, "Now the Lord is the Spirit, and where the Spirit of the Lord is, there is liberty." I receive my freedom now in Jesus' name!*

It is also written in Isaiah 45:2–3, "I will go before you and will level the mountains; I will break down gates of bronze and cut through bars of iron. I will give you the treasures of darkness, riches stored in secret places, so that you may know that I am the LORD, the God of Israel, who summons you by name" (NIV). Therefore I receive these promises and ask that the truth of the Word of God be fulfilled in my life from henceforth in Jesus' name. Thank You, Lord, for that which You have done in my life. In Jesus' mighty name I pray, amen.

About the Author's Ministry

Kingdom for the Forceful Ministries is dedicated to effecting a positive change in the way many believers pray, by providing Holy Spirit-inspired, Bible-based, power-packed prayer points that are set to produce tremendous results and bring glory to the Almighty. We are also here to encourage believers to be courageous, steadfast in faith, persevere in the face of persecution, endure hardship, and forcefully advance God's kingdom here on earth by providing materials such as inspiring books and devotionals.

For more information, please visit

www.kingdomfortheforceful.com